LIFE APPLICATION BIBLE COMMENTARY

life

APPLICATION®
Bible Commentary

1 & 2 THESSALONIANS

Bruce B. Barton, D.Min.
Linda Chaffee Taylor
David R. Veerman, M.Div.
Neil Wilson, M.R.E.

TYNDALE HOUSE
PUBLISHERS, INC.
CAROL STREAM,
ILLINOIS

GENERAL EDITOR: Grant Osborne, Ph.D.
SERIES EDITOR: Philip W. Comfort, D. Litt. et Phil.

Visit Tyndale's exciting Web site at www.tyndale.com.

Life Application Bible Commentary: 1 & 2 Thessalonians

Copyright © 1999 by The Livingstone Corporation. All rights reserved.

Contributing Editors: James C. Galvin, Ed.D., and Ronald A. Beers

Cover photograph of bridge and path copyright © by Alyn Stafford / iStockphoto. All rights reserved.

Cover photographs of woman with a laptop and man holding a pen copyright © by Dan Wilton / iStockphoto. All rights reserved.

Cover photo of man reading copyright © by Ronnie Comeau / iStockphoto. All rights reserved.

Interior illustrations of sun (1 Thessalonians) and spider (2 Thessalonians) copyright © 2004 by Tracy Walker. All rights reserved.

Scripture taken from the Holy Bible, *New International Version,*® *NIV.*® Copyright © 1973, 1978, 1984 by Biblica, Inc.™ Used by permission of Zondervan. All rights reserved worldwide. www.zondervan.com.

Scripture quotations marked NKJV are taken from the New King James Version. Copyright © 1979, 1980, 1982 by Thomas Nelson, Inc. Used by permission. All rights reserved.

Scripture quotations marked NRSV are taken from the New Revised Standard Version of the Bible, copyright © 1989, Division of Christian Education of the National Council of the Churches of Christ in the United States of America. Used by permission. All rights reserved.

(No citation is given for Scripture text that is exactly the same wording in all three versions—NIV, NKJV, and NRSV.)

Scripture quotations marked KJV are taken from the *Holy Bible,* King James Version.

Scripture quotations marked NLT are taken from the *Holy Bible,* New Living Translation, copyright © 1996. Used by permission of Tyndale House Publishers, Inc., Carol Stream, Illinois 60188. All rights reserved.

TYNDALE, Life Application, New Living Translation, NLT, and Tyndale's quill logo are registered trademarks of Tyndale House Publishers, Inc.

Library of Congress Cataloging-in-Publication Data

Barton, Bruce B.
  1 & 2 Thessalonians: life application commentary / Bruce B. Barton, Linda
  Taylor, Dave Veerman; general editor, Grant Osborne.
     p.   cm.—(Life application Bible commentary)
  Includes bibliographical references (p.   ) and index.
  ISBN 978-0-8423-2862-3 (sc : alk. paper)
  1. Bible. N.T. Thessalonians—Commentaries. I. Taylor, Linda Chaffee, date.
II. Veerman, David. III. Osborne, Grant R. IV. Title. V. Title: 1 and 2
Thessalonians. VI. Series.
BS2725.3.B37   1999
227′.81077—dc21   98-45169

Printed in the United States of America

15
11 10   9   8

CONTENTS

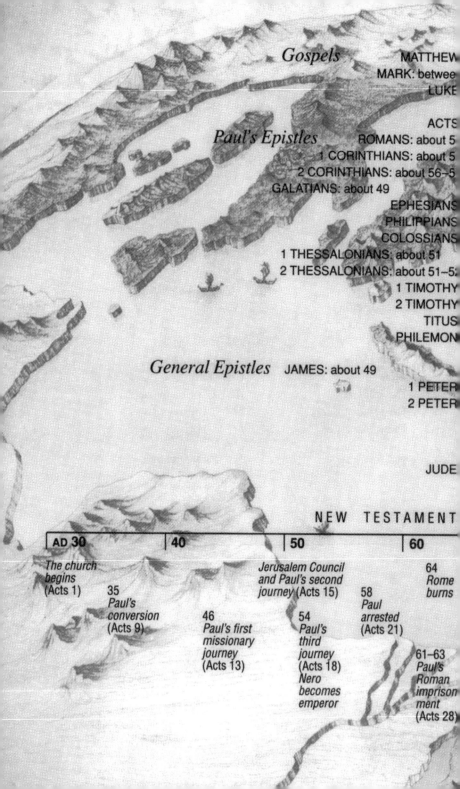

Gospels

MATTHEW
MARK: betwee
LUKE

ACTS
ROMANS: about 5
1 CORINTHIANS: about 5
2 CORINTHIANS: about 56–5
GALATIANS: about 49

Paul's Epistles

EPHESIANS
PHILIPPIANS
COLOSSIANS
1 THESSALONIANS: about 51
2 THESSALONIANS: about 51–5:
1 TIMOTHY
2 TIMOTHY
TITUS
PHILEMON

General Epistles   JAMES: about 49

1 PETER
2 PETER

JUDE

NEW   TESTAMENT

AD 30	40	50	60
The church begins (Acts 1)		*Jerusalem Council and Paul's second journey (Acts 15)*	64 *Rome burns*
	35 *Paul's conversion (Acts 9)*	58 *Paul arrested (Acts 21)*	
	46 *Paul's first missionary journey (Acts 13)*	54 *Paul's third journey (Acts 18) Nero becomes emperor*	61–63 *Paul's Roman imprison ment (Acts 28)*

etween 60–65
5–65
bout 60

JOHN: probably 80–85

bout 63–65

bout 61
bout 62
bout 61

bout 64
bout 66–67
bout 64
bout 61

HEBREWS: probably before 70

1 JOHN: between 85–90
2 JOHN: about 90
3 JOHN: about 90

bout 65

REVELATION: about 95

TIMELINE

|70 |80 |90 |100

67–68
Paul and
Peter
executed

68
Essenes hide
their library
of Bible
manuscripts
in a cave
in Qumran
by the
Dead Sea

Jerusalem
destroyed

About 75
John begins
ministry in
Ephesus

75
Rome begins
construction
of Colosseum

79 Mt. Vesuvius
erupts in Italy

About 98
John's
death
at Ephesus

FOREWORD

The Life Application Bible Commentary series provides verse-by-verse explanation, background, and application for every verse in the New Testament. In addition, it gives personal help, teaching notes, and sermon ideas that will address needs, answer questions, and provide insight for applying the Word of God to life today. The content is highlighted so that particular verses and phrases are easy to find.

Each volume contains three sections: introduction, commentary, and reference. The introduction includes an overview of the book, the book's historical context, a time line, cultural background information, major themes, an overview map, and an explanation about the author and audience.

The commentary section includes running commentary on the Bible text with reference to several modern versions, especially the New International Version, the New Revised Standard Version, and the New Living Translation, accompanied by life applications interspersed throughout. Additional elements include charts, diagrams, maps, and illustrations. There are also insightful quotes from church leaders and theologians such as John Calvin, Martin Luther, John Wesley, and A. W. Tozer. These features are designed to help you quickly grasp the biblical information and be prepared to communicate it to others. The reference section includes an index and a bibliography.

INTRODUCTION TO 1 THESSALONIANS

"You won't learn unless you ask questions!" Countless teachers and parents have explained that truth to children as they begin their educational experience. Those who desire to train others and impart knowledge don't mind responding to queries. Questions help them know what students are thinking and learning. Those who don't verbalize their doubts, voice their concerns, or seek to clarify what they have heard often harbor misunderstanding, go the wrong way, or live in ignorance.

Paul, master teacher, also felt like a father to believers in the churches he had planted on his missionary journeys. In both roles, he eagerly welcomed students' questions and patiently responded. With limited time in each location, however, Paul could not cover every topic, resolve every conflict, or answer every question, so he wrote letters to his beloved churches. Each letter had a purpose and spoke to specific needs.

Paul wrote this epistle, his first to the church at Thessalonica, to answer believers' questions and to commend them on their faith and commitment to Christ. The Thessalonians had questions . . . and they asked them. As you read this short, personal letter, look for answers for yourself. Also, think of questions that *you* will ask your spiritual mentor . . . and then learn.

AUTHOR

Paul (Saul of Tarsus): apostle of Christ, missionary, church planter, and gifted teacher.

The first verse of this letter identifies Paul as the author. Paul's traveling companions—Silas and Timothy—are mentioned as well, but Paul is clearly the primary author because the pronoun "I" is used so often: "When I could bear it no longer, I sent Timothy" (3:5 NLT).

As he had done on other occasions (see 1 Corinthians 16:21; Galatians 6:11; Colossians 4:18), Paul most likely dictated this letter to a scribe. Timothy, Paul's trusted assistant, may have been the one who actually transcribed the words. Also, Silas, who assisted Paul in founding the Thessalonian church, would have been very interested in this letter and may have offered suggestions on what to say.

At the end of this letter, however, Paul took ultimate responsibility for the contents when he again used the pronoun "I" in his final statement: "I command you in the name of the Lord to read this letter to all the brothers and sisters" (5:27 NLT).

Although critical scholars have challenged Paul as the author of most of the New Testament letters that bear his name, his authorship of 1 Thessalonians has been largely unchallenged (see the introduction for 2 Thessalonians). A few have suggested that Silas may have been the primary author of this letter because it does not reflect Paul's emphasis on law and grace (see Romans 5:1-21; 2 Corinthians 8:9; Galatians 3:18; 5:4). Instead, 1 Thessalonians focuses on the return of Christ (4:13–5:11). It may be true that Silas influenced the contents of this epistle, but he is not the primary author. Paul explicitly names himself as the authority behind this epistle (cf. 2:18 with 5:27). Early Christian writers, such as Irenaeus, Origen, and Eusebius, identified 1 Thessalonians as one of Paul's letters.

Paul's story. Ever since his dramatic conversion on the road to Damascus, Paul had been totally committed to Jesus and had taken every opportunity to proclaim him as the Messiah (Acts 9). In that blinding vision, Jesus called Paul to be a missionary evangelist. Before his conversion, Paul's goal had been to persecute Christians; since that life-changing moment, however, he focused on spreading the truth, the good news, about Jesus. During the next couple of decades, Paul traveled most of the Roman world, preaching to whomever would listen and establishing churches in the cities he visited. His message, however, was not always accepted. Jews opposed him in Damascus, Jerusalem, and just about every city and town he visited on his journeys, including Thessalonica.

Paul's missionary journeys began at Antioch (a city in present-day Turkey) in about A.D. 49 when the believers there commissioned him and Barnabas to take the gospel to distant cities. The two immediately set out and sailed to the island of Cyprus. They preached at Paphos and then sailed back to Asia Minor (present-day Turkey) to evangelize the cities of Perga, Attalia, Pisidian Antioch, Iconium, Lystra, and Derbe (Acts 13:4–14:28). They established churches in all of those cities.

A year later (A.D. 50), Paul set out on his second missionary journey. This time, however, he went without Barnabas because of a disagreement over Mark (Acts 15:36-41). Mark and Barnabas went to Cyprus. In Barnabas's place, Paul chose Silas, a respected member of the church in Jerusalem, to accompany him on his trip to the churches in Asia Minor (see Acts 15:40). On the

way, in Lystra, a young Greek believer named Timothy joined
Paul and Silas (Acts 16:1). Together the three traveled through
Asia Minor to Troas. Although Paul had planned to go farther
north, the group was hindered in some way (the Bible doesn't
reveal the details—Acts 16:7-8). While in Troas, God gave Paul a
vision in which a man begged him to come to Macedonia (northern Greece today). God's call was clear: Paul, Silas, and Timothy
were to leave and travel there. Without hesitation, they boarded
a ship and sailed across the choppy waters of the Aegean Sea to
the prosperous towns of the Macedonians—including the seaport
Thessalonica.

In Thessalonica Paul and his associates preached the gospel
courageously, just as they had been commissioned to do. Thessalonica had a large Jewish community and, thus, a synagogue.
Because Paul customarily ministered to the Jews first, he began
his ministry in each city at the synagogue: "As was Paul's custom, he went to the synagogue service, and for three Sabbaths
in a row he used the Scriptures to reason with the people" (Acts
17:2 NLT). As Paul taught about Jesus, emphasizing his suffering,
resurrection, and identity as the Messiah, some believed (Acts
17:3-4). The jealous Jewish leaders, however, stirred up "some
worthless fellows" to form an angry mob and sought Paul and
Silas at Jason's house. When they couldn't find Paul and Silas,
they seized Jason and some other believers and took them to the
city council, where they accused the Christians of treason (Acts
17:5-7). Paul's ministry in Thessalonica, therefore, was cut short.
He was forced to leave the infant church and travel to nearby
Berea. The Bereans "were more open-minded than those in
Thessalonica, and they listened eagerly to Paul's message. They
searched the Scriptures day after day to see if Paul and Silas were
teaching the truth" (Acts 17:11 NLT).

Because Paul's time in Thessalonica had been so limited, he was
concerned that he hadn't been able to teach the young believers the
details of Christian doctrine and to adequately model the Christian
faith. Later, when Timothy returned from Thessalonica with believers' questions, Paul wrote to encourage and instruct them.

AUDIENCE

The believers in Thessalonica.

The city of Thessalonica. Thessalonica was a bustling seaport on
the Aegean Sea. The Roman road that connected the major cities
of Macedonia—the Egnatian Way—was the main road through

Thessalonica. The Arch of Galerius, which spanned the Egnatian Way in Paul's day, still stands today.

In 315 B.C., Cassander, a military commander of Alexander the Great, founded the city and named it after his wife, Thessalonica, the half sister of Alexander the Great. The strategic location of the city allowed it to grow rapidly in wealth and influence. By 146 B.C., Thessalonica had been named the capital of Macedonia. The Romans even allowed the Thessalonians to govern themselves (in 42 B.C., Anthony and Octavia rewarded the city for supporting them in the Battle of Philippi by making it a free city). During Augustus's reign, Thessalonica was the most populous town in Macedonia. Thus, when Paul passed under the Arch of Galerius, he entered a city that was serving as the commercial and political center of Macedonia. Traders, merchants, Roman officials, and centurions walked the streets. Ships from throughout the Roman Empire filled its harbor.

Although Thessalonica had a sizable Jewish population, apparently they lived at peace with their Gentile neighbors, for when Paul spoke in the synagogue, many Gentiles responded to his message (Acts 17:2-4). Also, when the Jewish leaders turned against Paul and Silas, they took their case to the city council (Acts 17:6-7).

The church. As was his custom when beginning a ministry in any city, Paul went first to the Jews of Thessalonica. For three Sabbaths he taught in the synagogue, explaining the gospel and showing that Jesus was the Christ, the Messiah—the one about whom the prophets had foretold. Some were persuaded (Acts 17:1-4). Among these was Jason, who offered his home to the missionaries, and Aristarchus, who later became Paul's traveling companion (see Acts 19:29; 20:4; 27:2). A number of God-fearing Greeks (Greeks who attended the synagogue services) and prominent women of Thessalonica were also persuaded.

But the Jewish leaders of the synagogue grew jealous of Paul's success and thought he was stealing the prominent members of their congregation. In attempting to stop him, they rounded up some rough characters in the marketplace and started a riot in the city. The mob broke into Jason's house, looking for Paul and Silas. When they couldn't find them, they brought Jason before the city officials—*politarches* in Greek (Acts 17:6). This term was unknown in Greek literature until it was found on an inscription on the Vardar Gate in Thessalonica. The inscription dates from the first century and, therefore, is important evidence for the historicity of the Acts account.

The Jews accused Jason of housing preachers who had been

asserting that Jesus, instead of Caesar, was king (Acts 17:7).
Treason was a serious charge. The Romans didn't tolerate any
sign of defiance to their rule. Moreover the city officials probably
had heard of Claudius's recent expulsion of the Jews from Rome
(around A.D. 49). The historian Suetonius wrote that Claudius
threw the Jews out of Rome because of the "tumults instigated
by Chrestus" (see also Acts 18:1-2). Some scholars believe that
"Chrestus" is a misspelling of Christ; if so, the Jewish riots would
have occurred in response to the preaching of the gospel of Jesus
Christ. Although the city officials of Thessalonica probably didn't
understand why the Jews were rioting or whose fault it was,
they certainly had been apprised of the Jewish rioting that had
occurred throughout the Roman Empire and didn't want their city
to be thrown into turmoil.

Given the social instability of Thessalonica, the believers
decided to send Paul and Silas to nearby Berea. Paul's opponents
in Thessalonica were not so easily deterred and soon followed
Paul and Silas there, stirring up a riot against them in that city
as well (Acts 17:13). Once again Paul had to flee. This time, he
went to Athens—the center of Greek culture (Acts 17:15).

The church at Thessalonica was birthed in an atmosphere of
persecution. The band of believers had to withstand not only the
determined opposition of the Thessalonian Jews but also city
officials who could be manipulated by the Jews. The small group
who gathered around Paul was primarily made up of God-fearing
Greeks and former pagans (see Paul's description in 1:9).

The Thessalonian church was a gathering of enthusiastic new
believers. Within months, their courage, determination, eagerness,
and devotion had become well known. They still had much to
learn about the Christian faith, for Paul could only instruct them
for a short while. Yet their courage in the face of persecution
formed them into a church filled with extraordinary promise.

DATE AND SETTING

Written from Corinth around A.D. 51.

Paul and Silas's nighttime escape from Thessalonica inaugu-
rated their quick tour of Macedonia and Achaia (northern and
southern Greece, respectively). Their next stop was Berea, where
Timothy rejoined them. When Paul's enemies from Thessalonica
followed him there, he was quietly escorted to Athens. At this
intellectual center of the Greek world, Paul was allowed to present the gospel to the philosophers who had gathered at Mars Hill
(Acts 17:19-34). Although most of his audience rejected and even

mocked his message, a few were persuaded and became believers (Acts 17:32-34).

Silas and Timothy soon joined Paul there (Acts 17:15). While at Athens, Paul probably sent Timothy back to Thessalonica to see how the believers were doing (see Paul's reference to this in 3:1-4).

Paul traveled on to Corinth, where he found a receptive climate for his preaching. Ancient Corinth was one of the major cities of the Roman Empire. Its prominence and wealth were derived from the extraordinary amount of shipping and commerce that went through its harbors. Corinth's location on a four-and-a-half mile isthmus connecting mainland Greece and Achaia made it an ideal hub of shipping in the Roman Empire. Ships would be placed on wooden platforms and dragged across a stone road on the isthmus between the two ports of Corinth—Lechaeum and Cenchrea. As a commercial and cosmopolitan center, Corinth drew a substantial number of people from all over the Roman Empire.

Paul spent a full year and a half in Corinth, establishing a church in that city. During that time, Timothy returned from Thessalonica (Acts 18:5) with a favorable report on the Thessalonian believers and with their questions. In response to Timothy's report, Paul dictated 1 Thessalonians.

Paul's stay in Corinth can be dated with some precision because of the Delphi inscription. Dated A.D. 52, the inscription names Gallio as the proconsul of Achaia. A proconsul would rule for one year, beginning in July. Therefore, Gallio reigned from A.D. 51 to A.D. 52. During his ministry in Corinth, Paul appeared before Gallio to defend himself against certain charges (see Acts 18:12-16). This occurred toward the end of Paul's eighteen-month stay in the city. Beginning in A.D. 50, Paul's ministry in Corinth lasted to A.D. 51. Paul probably wrote 1 Thessalonians at the beginning of his stay—in A.D. 50.

OCCASION AND PURPOSE

To strengthen the Thessalonian Christians in their faith and assure them of Christ's return.

First Thessalonians is primarily a letter of praise and thanksgiving. In this letter Paul rejoiced over the Thessalonians' progress in the Christian faith. Timothy had given Paul an encouraging report on the Thessalonian believers. Their faith in Christ had remained strong (3:6). Although severely tested, they had withstood persecution (1:6). Having accepted Paul's message with great joy, they had been eagerly looking forward to Christ's return (1:6, 10). Their eager response was a clear sign that the Holy Spirit had been working in their hearts. This letter celebrates this great news (1:1-10; 2:13–3:13). Although Paul's ministry with them had been short, they had thrived. He wrote to congratulate them and to answer their questions about the faith.

As part of his instruction, Paul discussed the Second Coming. When presenting the gospel, Paul had told of Christ's return (1:10). Apparently, many Thessalonians were confused about the Second Coming and the fate of believers who had died. The Thessalonian believers probably understood Christ's return from their Greek perspective (the half-life after crossing the River Styx) and were therefore confused. Paul reassured them that all believers, living and dead, would share in the joy of Christ's return (4:13-17). He further explained that Christ's return would come suddenly (5:2), so they should be prepared (5:4-11).

Evidently, some had stopped working because they thought Christ would be returning at any moment. Paul redirected the enthusiasm of these young believers by outlining the proper way to await their Savior's return. "Stay alert" (5:6 NLT), continue to work (4:11), "encourage each other and build each other up" (5:11 NLT), he wrote.

Paul also took time to defend his ministry. Some had accused him and his co-workers of preaching for money and fame. This Paul vigorously denied (2:3-12).

The small and young Thessalonian church faced powerful and determined enemies. Paul wasn't concerned about the power of the enemies, however, as much as the strength of the Thessalonians' faith. Would they continue to seek God? Would they continue to love and encourage each other? Would they spurn the temptations of life in a cosmopolitan city? This letter explains exactly how the believers could endure persecution and opposition. They were to pray for each other, just as he was praying for them (1:2). They were to rejoice in each other's victories, just as he was rejoicing over them (1:3-10). They were to encourage each other to holy living, just as he had been encouraging them (4:1-4). Most of all, they were to seek strength from the Lord—from the one who could preserve them until Christ's sure return (5:23).

MESSAGE

Persecution; Paul's Ministry; Hope; Preparation for the Second Coming.

Persecution (1:6; 2:1-2, 14-16; 3:3-8). Paul and his associates had been hounded and finally driven out of Thessalonica during their short visit to that city. The new Christians Paul left behind were being persecuted because of their faith in Christ.

Importance for Today. Believers in any age can expect to be persecuted. They need to stand firm in their faith in the midst of trials,
being strengthened by the Holy Spirit, who helps them remain strong.

We may experience threats or overt slander and physical opposition, or the persecution and oppression may be more subtle.
Whatever the case, we must remain strong in faith through the
power of the Spirit, showing genuine love to others and maintain-
ing our moral character.

Paul's Ministry (1:5-6; 2:1-20; 3:1-8). Some in Thessalonica
were suggesting that Paul and his associates were preaching
with selfish motives. Paul denied these charges by reminding the
believers of his ministry among them and throughout the area.
Paul was determined to share the gospel despite being slandered
and facing other difficult circumstances.

Importance for Today. Paul not only delivered his message, he
also gave of himself. In addition, Paul didn't allow persecution or
slander to deter him from obeying the Lord and fulfilling his calling. In our ministries, we must become like Paul—faithful and
bold, yet sensitive and self-sacrificing.

Hope (1:3, 10; 2:19; 4:13-18). Paul encouraged the Thessalonian
Christians by reminding them that one day all believers, both those
who are alive and those who have died, will be united with Christ.
Christians who die before Christ's return have hope—the hope of
the resurrection of the body and life everlasting with the Lord.

Importance for Today. All who believe in Christ will live with
him forever. All those who belong to Jesus Christ—throughout
history—will be present with him at his second coming. No matter how bad the situation or bleak the outlook, we can take heart,
knowing that our future is secure in Christ. We can be confident
that at death or at the Second Coming, we will be with loved ones
who also have trusted in Christ.

**Preparation for the Second Coming (1:3, 9; 2:19-20; 3:13;
4:1-12; 5:1-28).** No one knows the time of Christ's return—it
will come suddenly, when people least expect it. Thus, believers
should live moral and holy lives, ever watchful for his coming,
not neglecting daily responsibilities, but always working and living to please the Lord.

Importance for Today. The gospel is not only what we believe
but also what we must live. The Holy Spirit helps us to be faithful to Christ, giving us strength to resist lust and fraud. Live as
though you expect Christ's return at any time. Don't be caught
unprepared.

VITAL STATISTICS

Purpose: To strengthen the Thessalonian Christians in their faith and give them the assurance of Christ's return

Author: Paul

To whom written: The church at Thessalonica and all believers everywhere

Date written: About A.D. 51 from Corinth; one of Paul's earliest letters

Setting: The church at Thessalonica was very young, having been established only two or three years before this letter was written. The Thessalonian Christians needed to mature in their faith. In addition, there was a misunderstanding concerning Christ's second coming—some thought Christ would return immediately, and thus they were confused when their loved ones died because they expected Christ to return beforehand. Also, believers were being persecuted.

Key verse: "Since we believe that Jesus died and was raised to life again, we also believe that when Jesus returns, God will bring back with him the believers who have died" (4:14 NLT).

Key people: Paul, Timothy, Silas

Key place: Thessalonica

Special features: Paul received from Timothy a favorable report about the Thessalonians. However, Paul wrote this letter to correct their misconceptions about the resurrection and the second coming of Christ.

OUTLINE

Paul and his companions were faithful to bring the gospel to the Thessalonians in the midst of persecution. The Thessalonians had only recently become Christians, and yet they had remained faithful to the Lord, despite the fact that the apostles were not with them. Others have been faithful in bringing God's Word to us. We must remain faithful and live in the expectation that Christ will return at any time.

1. Faithfulness to the Lord (1:1–3:13)
2. Watchfulness for the Lord (4:1–5:28)

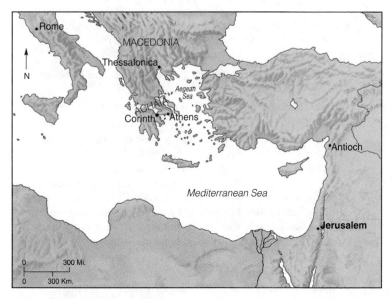

LOCATION OF THESSALONICA

Paul visited Thessalonica on his second and third missionary journeys. It was a seaport and trade center located on the Egnatian Way, a busy international highway. Paul probably wrote his two letters to the Thessalonians from Corinth.

1 Thessalonians 1

Paul and his companions probably arrived in Thessalonica in the
early summer of A.D. 50. They planted the first Christian church
in that city but had to leave in a hurry because their lives were
threatened (Acts 17:1-10). At the first opportunity, probably when
he stopped at Corinth, Paul sent Timothy back to Thessalonica to
see how the new believers were doing. Timothy returned to Paul
with good news: The Christians in Thessalonica were remaining
firm in the faith and were unified. But the Thessalonians did have
some questions about their new faith. Paul had not had time to
answer all their questions during his brief visit; in the meantime,
other questions had arisen. So Paul wrote this letter to answer
their questions and to commend them on their faithfulness to
Christ.

1:1 Paul, Silas and Timothy.[NIV] Paul began this letter by introducing
three men well known to the Thessalonian church—*Paul, Silas
and Timothy.* Paul (also called Saul), the head of this missionary
team and key writer of this letter, is first mentioned in Scripture
as standing beside coats while the Jewish leaders stoned the first
Christian martyr—Stephen: "Saul approved of their killing him"
(Acts 8:1 NRSV). Saul (Paul was probably his Roman surname,
Acts 13:9) was a Jew from the tribe of Benjamin (Romans 11:1),
raised as a strict Pharisee (Philippians 3:5), and educated under
a well-known teacher of the day, Gamaliel (Acts 22:3). Paul was
also a Roman citizen, a fact that helped him out several times
(Acts 22:27-29). After Stephen's death, Saul went on a vigorous
campaign to wipe out Christianity: "Saul was going everywhere
to destroy the church. He went from house to house, dragging out
both men and women to throw them into prison" (Acts 8:3 NLT).
But God had other plans for this zealous Jew—throwing him
from his horse on his way to Damascus and revealing to him that
Jesus truly was the Messiah (Acts 9:1-6). Saul's natural zeal and
passion were redirected toward the gospel message, for God had
chosen him for a special mission: "Saul is my chosen instrument

to take my message to the Gentiles and to kings, as well as to the people of Israel" (Acts 9:15 NLT). For more information on Paul, see the "Author" section of the introduction to this commentary.

Silas (sometimes called Silvanus) was a prophet (Acts 15:32) who was held in high esteem by the Jerusalem church. Silas accompanied Paul on his second missionary journey (Acts 15:36–17:15) and helped him establish the church in Thessalonica (Acts 17:1-9). Silas was one of the men chosen to deliver the important letter from the Jerusalem Council to the church in Antioch regarding Gentile inclusion in the church (Acts 15:22). He is mentioned by Paul in the salutation to both letters to the Thessalonians (here and in 2 Thessalonians 1:1), and he ministered with Timothy in Corinth (2 Corinthians 1:19).

The young Christian named Timothy joined Paul and Silas during Paul's second missionary journey. Paul and Barnabas had visited Timothy's hometown, Lystra, on the first missionary journey (Acts 14:8-21). At that time, Paul probably met Timothy, his mother, Eunice, and Timothy's grandmother Lois (who had previously become Christians), perhaps staying in their home. So when Paul and Silas returned there on the second missionary journey, Paul invited Timothy to join them. "Timothy was well thought of by the believers in Lystra and Iconium" (Acts 16:2 NLT). Timothy traveled the empire with Paul, preaching and teaching the Good News, as well as serving as Paul's assistant and sometimes as his emissary (3:2; Acts 19:22; 1 Corinthians 4:17; Philippians 2:19). Timothy and Silas also served together, staying behind to teach the believers while Paul moved on to unevangelized cities (Acts 17:14-15; 18:5). At one point, Timothy, like Paul, was imprisoned for his teaching (Hebrews 13:23).

This is a short introduction compared to Paul's other letters. Here he did not distinguish himself from these co-workers, even though he was an apostle and they were not. In many other letters, Paul introduced himself as "an apostle" (see Romans 1:1; 1 Corinthians 1:1; Galatians 1:1; Ephesians 1:1, among others). This probably indicates that the relationship between Paul and the Thessalonians was strong and that they were not doubting his apostleship (as was occurring in other places due to the infiltration of false teachers). Paul wrote letters to various churches to defend his message and ministry, but he did not do so in these letters to the Thessalonians. These are letters of encouragement and affirmation in the Christian faith.

To the church of the Thessalonians in God the Father and the Lord Jesus Christ.^{NIV} Paul and Silas had evangelized the city of Thessalonica. The account in the book of Acts describes

the preaching of Paul and Silas in that city and the conversion
of "many God-fearing Greek men and quite a few prominent
women" (Acts 17:4 NLT). Most likely, these God-fearing Greeks
were Jewish proselytes—Gentiles who had become converts
to Judaism and who believed in the one true God. From these
people came the converts to Christianity. Envious and angry Jewish leaders watched many from their synagogue follow Jesus
Christ. When a riot broke out, Paul and Silas had to leave under
cover of darkness. The Acts account mentions "three Sabbaths"
during which Paul preached in the synagogue (Acts 17:2 NLT),
but Paul probably was there for much longer than three weeks (a
time period that occurred between Acts 17:4 and 17:5). He had
to have been there long enough to do everything mentioned in
this letter *to the church of the Thessalonians,* such as work at his
trade (2:7-9), win converts, instruct new believers in the Christian
life (4:1-2), and form a strong bond of love with these believers
(2:17-20). Paul's letter to the Philippians indicates that he was in
Thessalonica long enough to receive financial help "more than
once" from the Philippians (Philippians 4:16 NLT).

Thessalonica was the capital and largest city (about two hundred thousand people) of the Roman province of Macedonia. The
most important Roman highway (the Egnatian Way)—extending
from Rome all the way to the Orient—went through Thessalonica. This highway, along with the city's thriving seaport, made
Thessalonica one of the wealthiest and most flourishing trade
centers in the Roman Empire. Recognized as a free city, Thessalonica was allowed self-rule and was exempted from most of the
restrictions placed by Rome on other cities in the empire. With its
international flavor, however, came many pagan religions and cultural influences that challenged the faith of the young Christians
there. (For more information on Thessalonica, see the "Setting"
and "Audience" sections of the introduction.)

Paul wrote to the "church" in Thessalonica. The Greek word
for church is *ekklesia,* meaning "assembly," and was not a dis-
tinctively Christian word. These people were part of the assembly
in Thessalonica that was *in God the Father and the Lord Jesus
Christ.* This set them apart from all the other assemblies that may
have been meeting in Thessalonica. This *ekklesia* was a religious
community committed to "God the Father" and to Jesus Christ as
their "Lord" (or Messiah). These characteristics distinguished the
assembly and reminded the Christians of who they were and what
they believed. They were a group united by their faith, set apart
from a sinful world, and committed to living out their Christianity
despite persecution and an immoral culture.

PAUL'S PRAYERS

Reference	*Paul prayed . . .*
Romans 10:1	that the Jews might be saved by believing in Jesus Christ.
2 Corinthians 13:7, 9	that the believers would not do anything wrong, but would pass the test and be made perfect in Christ.
Ephesians 1:17	that the believers would be given the Spirit of wisdom and revelation so that they would know God better.
Ephesians 3:16-19	that the believers would be filled with the Holy Spirit and experience God's love in its fullness.
Philippians 1:4, 9	that the believers' love for one another would abound more and more in knowledge, depth, and insight.
Colossians 1:9	that the believers would have a knowledge of God's will and be made wise with spiritual wisdom.
1 Thessalonians 3:10	that he and his co-workers could return to the believers and teach them further.
2 Thessalonians 1:11	that God would make the believers worthy of the life to which he called them, and that God would fulfill all their good intentions and faithful deeds.
Philemon 1:6	that Philemon would be active in sharing his faith.

Paul also requested that the believers pray for him:

Reference	*Paul requested . . .*
Romans 15:30-31	that they would join in his struggle for the churches, that he would be rescued from the Jews who persecuted him, and that the Christians in Jerusalem would accept the financial gift he was delivering from all the churches.
Ephesians 6:19-20	that God would give him the right words to share the Good News and that he would be able to keep on speaking boldly, despite his chains.
Colossians 4:3	that God would give him and his co-workers many opportunities to preach the Good News.
1 Thessalonians 5:25	that believers pray for him.
2 Thessalonians 3:1	that God's message would spread rapidly and be honored.
2 Thessalonians 3:2	that God would save them from wicked and evil people.

Grace and peace to you.[NIV] Letters at this time often would
begin by identifying the author, then the recipients, followed by a
greeting of peace. Paul usually added Christian elements, reminding his readers of their call by God. "Grace" means God's unmerited favor; "peace" refers to the peace that Christ made between
believers and God through his death on the cross. In these two
words of greeting Paul combined expressions from Jewish and
Gentile customs. Jews wished each other "peace" *(eirene* or the
Hebrew *shalom)*; Gentiles wished each other "grace" *(charis).*
When Christians used these words in greeting, the meaning was
significant. Christ offers grace in the form of life's great blessings
and the ability to handle difficulties; he offers peace that is an
inner calm no matter what the outward circumstances.

**1:2 We always thank God for all of you and pray for you
constantly.**[NLT] Many letters would follow the introduction with
a word of encouragement; Paul followed this pattern but only if
he truly meant it. Most of his letters *thank God* for the believers.
The letter to the Galatians is an exception. Paul there delved into
reprimand instead. Paul told the Thessalonians, a young church
facing persecution, that he and the other missionaries *always*
thanked God *for all of* them and prayed for them *constantly.* Paul
was not depending on his great skills or his teaching to carry
the young believers; instead, he was trusting in God to guide
and protect them. Paul spent much time traveling and preaching, but apparently he spent much time on his knees praying for
the believers. The chart describes some of his prayer topics and
requests. (See also the chart "Prayer in Paul's Life and Letters" in
the *Life Application Bible Commentary: Philippians, Colossians
& Philemon,* pages 24–25.)

**1:3 We continually remember before our God and Father your
work produced by faith, your labor prompted by love, and
your endurance inspired by hope in our Lord Jesus Christ.**[NIV]
The Thessalonian believers had stood firm when persecuted (1:6;
3:1-4, 7-8). Paul commended these young Christians for their
work, labor, and *endurance.* He and his companions *continually*
remembered these qualities *before our God and Father.* These
qualities might characterize any hardworking group of people,
so Paul described what he knew was the motivation behind their
work, labor, and endurance. It was *faith, hope,* and *love.* These
three qualities are foundational to Christian character (see 1 Corinthians 13:13).

The Thessalonians' work had been produced by faith. Paul
made it clear that believers are saved by faith alone (Ephesians
2:9) but that faith should produce good works in the life of each

FAITH, HOPE, AND LOVE

In our days of complex formulas, this simple program for Christian living still holds true. (Verses quoted from NIV. Italics added.)

Romans 5:1-5	"We have been justified through *faith*. . . . We rejoice in the *hope* of the glory of God. . . . God has poured out his *love* into our hearts by the Holy Spirit, whom he has given us."
1 Corinthians 13:13	"And now these three remain: *faith, hope* and *love*. But the greatest of these is *love.*"
Galatians 5:5-6	"But by *faith* we eagerly await through the Spirit the righteousness for which we *hope*. . . . The only thing that counts is *faith* expressing itself through *love.*"
Ephesians 1:15-18	"Ever since I heard about your *faith* . . . and your *love* . . . I have not stopped giving thanks. . . . I pray also that the eyes of your heart may be enlightened in order that you may know the *hope* to which he has called you."
Ephesians 4:2-5	". . . Bearing with one another in *love*. . . . You were called to one *hope* . . . one *faith.*"
Colossians 1:4-5	"Because we have heard of your *faith* in Christ Jesus and of the *love* you have for all the saints . . . that spring from the *hope* that is stored up for you in heaven."
1 Thessalonians 5:8	"Let us be self-controlled, putting on *faith* and *love* as a breastplate, and the *hope* of salvation as a helmet."
Hebrews 10:22-24	"Let us draw near to God with a sincere heart in full assurance of *faith*. . . . Let us hold unswervingly to the *hope* we profess. . . . Let us consider how we may spur one another on toward *love* and good deeds."
1 Peter 1:3-8	"Praise be to the God and Father of our Lord Jesus Christ! . . . He has given us new birth into a living *hope* . . . who through *faith* are shielded by God's power until the coming of the salvation. . . . Though you have not seen him, you *love* him."
1 Peter 1:21-22	"Your *faith* and *hope* are in God. . . . Have sincere *love* for your brothers, *love* one another deeply, from the heart."

believer. Faith is not meant to be practiced in a vacuum; instead, believers are to do good works. They work not *to be* saved but *because* they are saved. The work is for the kingdom of God. The character of that work will be different for every believer, but the motivation (faith) and the desire (to bring more people to saving faith) are the same. Paul was pointing not to any specific "work" but rather to the fact that the believers were working for the kingdom. (This probably softened Paul's later admonition to those who were not doing this but instead were being lazy—2 Thessalonians 3:6-15.) To do "work produced by faith" does not mean that new believers have to leave their jobs and become full-time Christian workers. Believers can work for the kingdom in almost any vocation, for as they rub shoulders with nonbelievers, they can have a positive impact for Christ. Their faith in him prompts their work for him in their present vocations.

The Thessalonians' labor had been prompted by love. Because of their love, believers are willing to *labor.* The Greek word translated "labor" is *kopos,* meaning toil and hardship. The Greek word translated "love" is *agape,* a self-sacrificing love. The believers were willing to give of themselves (even if it meant hardship) in service to others. Only God's kind of love could prompt such willing labor. (For more on this concept, see the commentary on Titus 3:8 in *Life Application Bible Commentary: 1 & 2 Timothy / Titus,* page 282, and the chart "What God Wants Us to Do for Others" in *Life Application Bible Commentary: Galatians,* page 200.)

THESE THREE
Faith, hope, and love are anchors for the Christian life. Paul described how the Thessalonians' faith led to work, their love led to labor, and their hope led to endurance. These characteristics ought to be seen in all believers. Too often, however,

- a believer claims to have *faith* in Jesus Christ as Lord but is not motivated to *work* to promote his kingdom or the spread of the gospel;
- a believer claims to *hope* in Jesus Christ as the one in control of his or her life, but when faced with difficulty or disappointment, he or she does not *endure* in the faith and turns away;
- a believer claims to *love* Jesus Christ, but when serving in Christ's kingdom becomes *labor,* he or she backs off.

Faith, hope, and love must result in work, labor, and endurance that will guide all believers through life—showing what to do and how to do it. How are your faith, hope, and love being shown?

Finally, the Thessalonians' endurance had been inspired by hope in the Lord Jesus Christ. The Greek word translated "endurance" or "steadfastness" *(hypomone)* refers not to passive acceptance but to strong fortitude in the face of opposition or difficulty (see also Romans 12:12; Hebrews 10:32; 1 Peter 2:20). Enduring persecution is one of the main themes of this first chapter. Paul's readers had remained faithful even though they had faced serious opposition and persecution from the citizens of Thessalonica (1:6; 2:14). The reason for this strength? *Hope in our Lord Jesus Christ.* Most likely this refers to Christ's second coming. This "hope" is not a vague desire that he will return but a certainty that believers look forward to during their lives on this earth. That hope makes it possible for them to endure all manner of difficulty and hardship—even persecution because of their faith—because they know that God sees all and one day will make everything right.

1:4 **For we know, brothers and sisters beloved by God, that he has chosen you.**^{NRSV} Paul, Silas, and Timothy could resolutely say to the believers in Thessalonica (their *brothers and sisters beloved by God*), "We know . . . that he has chosen you." In the following verses they will explain how they know that these believers had been chosen by God.

That God chooses his people forms the basis of the doctrine of election—defined as God's choice of an individual or group for a specific purpose or destiny. The doctrine of election teaches that believers are saved only because of God's grace and mercy, not on their own merit. God does not save anyone because that person deserves to be saved; rather, he graciously and freely gives salvation to whomever he chooses. No one can influence God's decision; it all happens according to his plan. No one can take pride in or credit for his or her salvation.

The doctrine of election runs through the Bible, beginning with God's choosing Abraham's descendants as his special people. Through them, God would fulfill his promise to Abraham that "in you all the families of the earth shall be blessed" (Genesis 12:3 NKJV). Listen to the words of Moses:

> *For you are a people holy to the LORD your God. The LORD your God has chosen you out of all the peoples on the face of the earth to be his people, his treasured possession. The LORD did not set his affection on you and choose you because you were more numerous than other peoples, for you were the fewest of all peoples. But it was because the LORD loved you and kept the oath he swore to your forefathers that he brought you out with a mighty hand and redeemed you from the land of slavery, from the power of Pharaoh king of Egypt. . . . Therefore, take care to follow the commands, decrees and laws I give you today.* (Deuteronomy 7:6-8, 11 NIV)

Israel fulfilled a specific purpose: it was the nation into which the Savior, Jesus Christ, was born as a human being. Being chosen or elected connotes special status. Israel had been chosen by God to inherit the land, receive his Word, and then convey that Word to all the nations. The nation did not follow the commandments that Moses had given them from God, however, so they wound up in exile because of their sins. After the nation went into exile, the prophets told the people that God had chosen a "remnant" (a small group) of true believers who would remain after the Exile (see, for example, Isaiah 10:20-22; 37:31-32; Jeremiah 42:2; Micah 2:12; 5:7-8; Zephaniah 3:12-13; Haggai 1:14; Zechariah 8:6, 12).

CHOSEN IN HIM

Paul reminded the Thessalonians of their status as God's chosen ones. Very few issues cause more confusion and even arguments among Christians than the issue of election (being chosen by God). It is very difficult to simultaneously embrace God's sovereignty and humans' responsibility. Election was not a theological concept dreamed up by Paul; it appears throughout Scripture. Even though we may not be able to completely comprehend how these two truths can coexist, we can say this:

Being chosen . . .
- comes from the heart of God, not the mind of people;
- should be an incentive to please God, not to ignore him;
- should give birth to gratitude, not complacency.

Human responsibility . . .
- requires that we actively confess Christ as Lord;
- focuses on living according to God's plan;
- requires that we share the gospel with everyone.

Having been chosen by God energizes a Christian's life of obedient service. Responsibility challenges us to build a life worthy of God's choice. As you consider God's divine selection of you, how do you respond—with pride or apathy or with a worshipful heart and obedience?

Even many among this remnant of Jews eventually would turn away. Although the Jews were chosen as special recipients and emissaries of God's grace, their opportunity to participate in that plan arrived with the coming of Christ, their promised Messiah. But many didn't recognize Christ and so rejected him. As John wrote: "He came to his own people, and even they rejected him. But to all who believed him and accepted him, he gave the right to become children of God" (John 1:11-12 NLT). The "all who believed" Jesus included Jews and Gentiles alike. Thus, God's *chosen* and elected people are now the Christians, the body of Christ, the church—all who believe on, accept, and receive Jesus Christ as Messiah, Savior, and Lord. The church has now replaced unbelieving Israel (those persecuting the Christians) as the "chosen." Jesus himself called his followers the "chosen ones" (NLT) or the "elect" (NIV) in Matthew 24:22, 24, 31; Mark 13:20, 22, 27.

In Ephesians 1:4-5, Paul wrote, "Even before he made the world, God loved us and chose us in Christ to be holy and without fault in his eyes. God decided in advance to adopt us into his own family by bringing us to himself through Jesus Christ" (NLT). In 2 Thessalonians 2:13-14, Paul wrote to these believers, "We are always thankful that God chose you to be among the first to experience salvation—a salvation that came through the Spirit who makes you holy and through your belief in the truth. He called you to salvation when we told you the Good News; now you can share in the glory of our Lord Jesus Christ" (NLT).

Being chosen is a Christian's highest privilege.

1:5 Because our gospel came to you not simply with words, but also with power, with the Holy Spirit and with deep conviction.[NIV] The word had been chosen by God because his presentation of the gospel brought great results. Paul and his companions had brought the message to Thessalonica. There were no believers when they arrived; when they left, a strong church had been planted. This was not a source of pride for the missionaries, however. When Paul brought the gospel message to people, he spoke with *words,* and God used those words to ignite the Thessalonians to understand and believe that message. God had used Paul's words by enveloping them in divine *power* (see also 1 Corinthians 2:1-5; Ephesians 6:17-18). Paul's words alone could not persuade anyone to believe or open a needy heart to hear the message. But his words combined with the power of the *Holy Spirit* to convince, enlighten, and comfort the listeners could help many to believe what Paul was saying and give their hearts and lives to Christ for salvation. This "power" may also have included miracles (see Acts 14:3; 16:17-18; 19:11-12; Romans 15:17-19; 2 Corinthians 12:12).

Who is the Holy Spirit? God is three persons in one—the Father, the Son, and the Holy Spirit. God became a man in Jesus so that Jesus could die for our sins. Jesus rose from the dead to offer salvation to all people through spiritual renewal and rebirth. When Jesus ascended into heaven, he left the earth, but he promised to send the Holy Spirit so that his spiritual presence would still be among mankind (see Luke 24:49). The Holy Spirit first became available to all believers at Pentecost (Acts 2). Whereas in Old Testament days the Holy Spirit empowered specific individuals for specific purposes, now all believers have the power of the Holy Spirit available to them. For more on the Holy Spirit, read John 14:16-28; 15:26-27; Romans 8:9; 1 Corinthians 12:13; and 2 Corinthians 1:22.

The words "deep conviction" refer to the profound conviction or assurance of those who brought the message—they were convicted and convinced of the truth of the gospel. So much so that not only did they travel around the world to share the message, but they lived every day in the power of that message. Paul continued: **And you know of our concern for you from the way we lived when we were with you.**^{NLT} The last half of this verse points to chapter 2, where Paul discusses his ministry with them. The Thessalonians could see that what Paul, Silas, and Timothy were preaching was true because these men lived it. They demonstrated their willingness to face opposition, travel under adverse conditions, and work without being paid while dealing with severe frustrations.

THE SPIRIT'S POWER
Paul presented the gospel with the Holy Spirit's power. The Holy Spirit changes people when they believe the gospel. When we tell others about Christ, we must depend on the Holy Spirit to open their eyes and convince them that they need salvation. God's power—not our cleverness or persuasion—changes people. Without the work of the Holy Spirit, our words are meaningless. The Holy Spirit not only convicts people of sin but also assures them of the truth of the gospel. Trust the Holy Spirit to work in the hearts of those with whom you share the Good News. He will work his way and in his timing. You must simply be a willing instrument in the Father's hand.

1:6 So you received the message with joy from the Holy Spirit in spite of the severe suffering it brought you. In this way, you imitated both us and the Lord.^{NLT} The *message* of salvation, though welcomed with great *joy,* brought the Thessalonian believers *severe suffering* because it led to persecution from both Jews and Gentiles (3:2-4; Acts 17:5). This was to be expected, however, for Jesus himself had said,

> *If the world hates you, remember that it hated me first. The world would love you as one of its own if you belonged to it, but you are no longer part of the world. I chose you to come out of the world, so it hates you. . . . Since they persecuted me, naturally they will persecute you. . . . They will do all this to*

CALLED TO SUFFER

The New Testament abounds with predictions concerning suffering and words of comfort for those who are suffering.

Speaker	Reference	Words about Suffering
Jesus	Matthew 5:10-12	Those who are persecuted are called "blessed."
Jesus	John 15:20	Jesus was persecuted; we will be persecuted.
The Apostles	Acts 5:41	We can rejoice for being considered worthy to suffer for Christ.
Jesus	Acts 9:16	Paul was called by God to suffer for Jesus' name.
Paul	Romans 8:17	As children and heirs, we will share in Jesus' suffering.
Paul	2 Corinthians 1:3-7	God gives comfort in suffering.
Paul	2 Corinthians 4:7-12	Paul suffered so that others might be saved.
Paul	2 Corinthians 6:4-5, 9-10	Paul suffered yet rejoiced.
Paul	Ephesians 3:13	Our sufferings can glorify God.
Paul	Philippians 1:29	Suffering for Christ's name is a privilege.
Paul	2 Timothy 1:12	We must not be ashamed when we suffer.
Paul	2 Timothy 2:10	Paul suffered for the sake of other believers.
Paul	2 Timothy 3:11	God will rescue us from suffering—now or in eternity.
Paul	2 Timothy 4:5	We are called to endure hardship.
Author of Hebrews	Hebrews 10:32-34	We can face suffering because we know we have God's inheritance.
James	James 1:2	We can consider it pure joy to face trials.
Peter	1 Peter 1:6-7	Our suffering is refining our faith.
Peter	1 Peter 2:21	We suffer because Christ suffered.
Peter	1 Peter 3:13-14	We are blessed for suffering for what is right.
Peter	1 Peter 4:1, 13, 16	We suffer yet rejoice because we suffer for Christ.
Jesus	Revelation 2:10	We must be faithful, even to death; the crown of life awaits us.

*you because of me, for they have rejected the one who sent
me. . . . I have told you all this so that you may have peace in
me. Here on earth you will have many trials and sorrows. But
take heart, because I have overcome the world.* (John 15:18-21;
16:33 NLT)

Jesus had told his disciples that because he suffered, so would
they. The disciples had already faced much suffering: Just before
coming to Thessalonica, Paul and Silas had been beaten and
imprisoned in Philippi (Acts 16:16-40). Paul faced "severe suffering" during much of his ministry (some of these sufferings are
recorded in 2 Corinthians 11:16-33). So when the Thessalonian
believers suffered for their faith, they were in good company.
Through that suffering, they *imitated* the missionaries and *the
Lord* himself (2:14).

First Thessalonians 1:6 is the second reference to the Holy
Spirit in two verses. The same Holy Spirit who gave power to the
words of the gospel message also opened hearts to receive the
message and then gave joy to the hearers. The Holy Spirit works
in those presenting the message and those hearing and accepting
it. He gives "joy" (see Galatians 5:22).

The New Testament places strong emphasis on imitating leaders. It also gives strong words to those leaders that they be worthy
of emulation (Scripture quotations are from the NIV):

- Jesus told his followers to learn from his example of gentleness
  and humility.

  Matthew 11:29—"Take my yoke upon you and learn from me."

- Paul urged believers to follow his example.

  1 Corinthians 11:1—"Follow my example, as I follow the
    example of Christ."
  Philippians 3:17—"Join with others in following my example,
    brothers, and take note of those who live according to the
    pattern we gave you."
  Philippians 4:9—"Whatever you have learned or received or
    heard from me, or seen in me—put it into practice."

- The new Christians at Thessalonica received training in
  discipleship from Paul, and even in suffering, they modeled
  before others what they had learned.

  1 Thessalonians 1:6-7—"You became imitators of us and
    of the Lord; in spite of severe suffering, you welcomed
    the message with the joy given by the Holy Spirit. And so
    you became a model to all the believers in Macedonia and
    Achaia."

- Paul used his unworthiness to receive Christ as an example of grace so that no one would hold back from coming to Christ.

  1 Timothy 1:16—"But for that very reason I was shown mercy so that in me, the worst of sinners, Christ Jesus might display his unlimited patience as an example for those who would believe on him and receive eternal life."

- The writer of Hebrews wanted the believers to imitate the faith of their leaders. People did not have Bibles to read as they do today, so they had to look at other sources. Hopefully their leaders were worthy of emulation.

  Hebrews 13:7—"Remember your leaders, who spoke the word of God to you. Consider the outcome of their way of life and imitate their faith."

- Peter taught Christian leaders to lead by example, not by commands.

  1 Peter 5:3—"Not lording it over those entrusted to you, but being examples to the flock."

TOO SEVERE
Many think that pain is the exception in the Christian life. When suffering occurs, they say, "Why me?" They feel as though God deserted them, or perhaps they accuse him of not being as dependable as they thought he should be. In reality, the world is sinful, so even believers suffer. God allows some Christians to become martyrs for the faith, and he allows others to survive persecution. Rather than asking, "Why me?" we should ask, "Why not me?" Our faith and the values of this world are on a collision course. If we expect pain and suffering to come, we will not be shocked when they occur. But we can also take comfort in knowing that Jesus also suffered. He understands our fears, our weaknesses, and our disappointments (see Hebrews 2:16-18; 4:14-16). He promised never to leave us (Matthew 28:18-20), and he intercedes on our behalf (Hebrews 7:24-25). In times of pain, persecution, or suffering, trust confidently in Christ.

1:7-10 So that you became an example to all the believers in Macedonia and in Achaia.[NRSV] The Thessalonians had followed the example of the missionaries and of the Lord himself (1:6), and they, in turn, had become *an example to all the believers in Macedonia and in Achaia.* Paul praised this church (no other church received this particular type of praise) because not only were they model believers to an unbelieving world, but they were also examples to other believers. "Macedonia" and "Achaia" refer to the two provinces that made up Greece—and the area where most of the new churches were concentrated, for Paul had planted many of them. Yet Paul went even further, writing that **the Lord's message rang out from you not only in Macedonia and Achaia—your faith in God has become known everywhere.**NIV These Thessalonian believers had a world-wide reputation and were an example to all the other churches. "The Lord's message" refers to the gospel—the Good News of salvation. The Thes-

> Joy is the standard that flies on the battlements of the heart when the King is in residence.
> *R. Leonard Small*

salonians believed it, lived it, and shared it. Indeed, Paul pictured it as ringing out like a bell or the sound of a trumpet, resounding across the continent. The message of these believers' lives had an effect that reached even farther than the boundaries of "Macedonia and Achaia" (Greece)—their *faith* was *known everywhere* (literally "in every place"). This probably means that the Thessalonians' reputation had spread to every place (locality) where a church had been established.

FOLLOW THE LEADER
Paul stressed the importance of the Thessalonians' being an example to others. They had been faithful under pressure of opposition. Their persistence had encouraged and inspired others. Their witness had been courageous even while they were suffering. We are responsible for the example we set. We must not live with only our own survival in mind. Others will follow our example, and we have a responsibility to them if we claim to live for Christ. Does your example make it easier for others to believe, follow, and mature in Christ? Or would those who follow you end up confused and misled?

Therefore we do not need to say anything about it, for they themselves report what kind of reception you gave us. They tell how you turned to God from idols to serve the living and true God, and to wait for his Son from heaven, whom he raised from the dead—Jesus, who rescues us from the coming wrath.NIV So well known was the Thessalonians' faith that Paul did *not need to say anything about it.* Other people brought it up first! Any believer from any church might be found talking about what was going on in Thessalonica. Their faith was universally known. And so, apparently, was the *kind of reception* the Thessalonians had given to the missionaries. The other churches knew how some in Thessalonica had *turned to God from idols to serve the living and true God.* In fact, they were suffering severely for this change of faith and life (1:6). They had turned from dead, worthless idols to serve the one "living and true God." The impact of this may slip past modern ears. The idols, the Greek "gods," were considered to be extremely powerful. All power of all kinds rested with any number of gods. And there were many of them— readers of Greek mythology are acquainted with the gods of ancient Greece. For these Thessalonians, living barely fifty miles from Mount Olympus, where the Greek gods were said to live, to turn from their many false idols to the one true God had caused upheaval in all areas of their lives. No wonder they faced persecution. Not only had they turned, but they had allowed this message to so impact their lives that they were willing to "serve the living and true God"—no matter what the sacrifice.

In addition to turning and serving, the Thessalonians were waiting. The Christian life doesn't end at death. All believers await God's *Son from heaven, whom he raised from the dead— Jesus, who rescues us from the coming wrath.* All believers look forward to the Second Coming when Jesus Christ, who rose from the dead, will return and will take his followers to be with him. Thus he will rescue them from "the coming wrath," referring to when God will destroy all evil (see 5:9; 2 Thessalonians 1:6-10). This "coming wrath" has been a difficult concept for many to accept; yet it is a reality that God will indeed bring wrath upon a sinful world. Just as in the Old Testament the people understood God's hand in all matters—both blessings and curses—so it was in the New Testament, as noted in the following verses (quoted from the NLT):

- John 3:36: "And anyone who believes in God's Son has eternal life. Anyone who doesn't obey the Son will never experience eternal life but remains under God's angry judgment."
- Romans 1:18: "But God shows his anger from heaven against all sinful, wicked people who suppress the truth by their wickedness."
- Romans 9:22: "In the same way, even though God has the right to show his anger and his power, he is very patient with those on whom his anger falls, who are destined for destruction."
- Ephesians 5:6: "Don't be fooled by those who try to excuse these sins, for the anger of God will fall on all who disobey him."
- Colossians 3:5-6: "So put to death the sinful, earthly things lurking within you. Have nothing to do with sexual immorality, impurity, lust, and evil desires. Don't be greedy, for a greedy person is an idolater, worshiping the things of this world. Because of these sins, the anger of God is coming."
- Revelation 11:18: "The nations were filled with wrath, but

now the time of your wrath has come. It is time to judge the dead and reward your servants the prophets, as well as your holy people, and all who fear your name, from the least to the greatest. It is time to destroy all who have caused destruction on the earth."

- Revelation 14:19: "So the angel swung his sickle over the earth and loaded the grapes into the great winepress of God's wrath."
- Revelation 19:15-16: "From his mouth came a sharp sword to strike down the nations. He will rule them with an iron rod. He will release the fierce wrath of God, the Almighty, like juice flowing from a winepress. On his robe at his thigh was written this title: King of all kings and Lord of all lords."

God's wrath is a certainty, for he will not let sin continue unabated forever. Believers, however, can trust in their Savior, who rescues them.

Paul emphasized Christ's second coming throughout this book. Because the Thessalonian church was being persecuted, Paul encouraged them to look forward to the deliverance that Christ would bring. A believer's hope is in the return of Jesus, the "great God and Savior" (Titus 2:13 NLT). Just as surely as Christ was raised from the dead and ascended into heaven, he will return (Acts 1:11).

TURN, SERVE, WAIT
The Thessalonians responded to the Lord's message whole-heartedly. All of us should respond to the Good News as the Thessalonians did: *Turn* to God, *serve* God, and *wait* for his Son, Christ, to return from heaven.

- We should *turn* from sin to God because Christ is coming to judge the earth. Have you turned to God? If so, from what? What difference has it made in your life?
- We should be fervent in our *service* because we have little time before Christ returns. Are you serving God? If so, how? Is he pleased with your work for him?
- We should be *waiting* for Christ to return and always be ready because we don't know when he will come. Do you eagerly await the coming of Christ from heaven? Why or why not?

---

1 Thessalonians 2

PAUL REVIEWS HIS RELATIONSHIP WITH THE THESSALONIANS / 2:1-20

Paul and Silas had been driven out of Thessalonica by their enemies, who then slandered Paul to the young believers in the new church there. This letter answers the accusations of Paul's enemies by describing what the believers already knew—the truth of Paul and Silas's message, the sincerity of their motives, and the proof of both by their actions among them. Paul was totally committed to the growth of those who had come to faith through his preaching.

2:1 You yourselves know, dear brothers and sisters, that our visit to you was not a failure.^{NLT} This refers to Paul's first *visit* to Thessalonica recorded in Acts 17:1-10. The ministry in Thessalonica had begun calmly enough, but it had ended with Paul and Silas leaving under cover of darkness because a riotous mob of Jewish leaders and "worthless fellows" was attempting to turn the city against them. And the Jews' slander did not end after Paul and Silas had left the city. Not only did the Jews follow them to Berea to stir up trouble there (Acts 17:13), but evidently they continued to speak against the missionaries to the Thessalonian believers. The Jews seem to have taken the occasion of Paul and Silas's hasty departure to try to convince the believers that they had been defrauded. In the following verses Paul offers a response to what the Jews had said against him and Silas.

FROM DEFEAT TO VICTORY
Viewed from the beginning effort, Paul's ministry in Thessalonica was apparently a failure, but it didn't end that way. What began as a withdrawal from Thessalonica produced great victory later. How do you handle major defeats? How do you react when you suffer a major loss? The next time your efforts of ministry appear thwarted or futile, don't despair. Remind yourself that God is in control even if it doesn't feel like it at the moment. Trust him for the final result. Ask him to show you what you need to do, and see what you can learn from the situation.

Some may have thought that the visit to Thessalonica was
a failure, but the believers there knew that it *was not a failure*
(meaning ineffective or worthless). Paul and Silas had arrived in
a city with no believers. They left a strong church that was alive,
growing, standing up to persecution, and becoming an example to
believers across the world. Lives had been changed. Obviously,
Paul and Silas's visit had not been a "failure."

**2:2 You know how badly we had been treated at Philippi just
before we came to you and how much we suffered there. Yet
our God gave us the courage to declare his Good News to you
boldly, in spite of great opposition.**^{NLT} The Thessalonians knew
that Paul and Silas had indeed been treated *badly* in *Philippi.*
Just before coming to Thessalonica, Paul and Silas had visited
the city of Philippi, where they had met a group of women who
were meeting for prayer outside the city. One of them, Lydia,
became a believer and insisted that Paul and Silas stay at her
home. One day Paul and Silas were accosted by a demon-
possessed slave girl who yelled at them. She continued to do this
day after day whenever she saw them. Finally, Paul spoke to the
demon and forced it to leave the girl. Although the girl had been
set free of the demon, her masters were angry that she could no
longer make money for them by telling fortunes. They formed
a mob, and Paul and Silas "were severely beaten [with wooden
rods], and then they were thrown into prison" with "their feet
in the stocks" (Acts 16:23-24). In Philippi the missionaries had
indeed *suffered.*

Despite severe suffering for sharing the good news of Christ,
Paul explained that God had given him *courage* to go on to Thessalonica and *declare [God's] Good News . . . boldly.* This "courage" did not come from within Paul but was given to him by
God. Only such supernatural courage could help the men boldly
face persecution because the threat of opposition had not been
left behind in Philippi. The missionaries continued to encounter
great opposition. In Thessalonica, their enemies had started a riot
against Paul and Silas and their teachings. The Jewish leaders had
claimed that Paul and Silas were "guilty of treason against Caesar" because they were professing "allegiance to another king,
named Jesus" (Acts 17:7 NLT). In reality, their only "crime" was
proclaiming the good news of salvation in Jesus Christ. In addition, some Jews in Thessalonica had sent a delegation to Berea
to follow Paul and Silas in order to stir up trouble against them
(Acts 17:13).

DYNAMIC DUO
Paul and Silas preached boldly even when facing opposition. Boldness is not reckless impulsiveness. Boldness requires courage to press through fears and do what is right. How can we be more bold? Like the apostles, we need to pray for that courage. To gain boldness, you can (1) pray for the power of the Holy Spirit to give you courage, (2) look for opportunities in your family and neighborhood to talk about Christ, (3) realize that rejection, social discomfort, and embarrassment are not persecution, and (4) start where you are by being bolder in small ways.

2:3 So you can see that we were not preaching with any deceit or impure motives or trickery.[NLT] The words "so you can see" seem to indicate that Paul was answering accusations. Perhaps some of the Jews who had caused the riot in Thessalonica had told the Thessalonian believers that Paul and Silas had been defrauding them (Acts 17:5-6). But Paul pointed out that he had just left severe persecution in Philippi before his arrival in Thessalonica. Then he had experienced persecution in Thessalonica, causing him and Silas to leave secretly. How then could they have been preaching with any other motive than to obey God? If they had wanted to make money and please the crowds with their preaching, they had certainly gone about it the wrong way! Instead, they had faced persecution and then, with courage (2:2), had faced more persecution. No preacher hoping for an easy buck and popularity would take such a path. People only suffer willingly for something they believe in totally. Such was the case for Paul.

Paul mentioned three ways in which he and his companions *were not preaching.* First, they did not preach *with any deceit.* They were not trying to lead the Thessalonians down the wrong path. They had spoken the truth and had suffered for it. Although they had been accused of telling lies, Paul knew that he had preached only the truth.

Second, they did not preach with *impure motives.* The word "impure" may point to accusations of sexual sin or sensuality, a trait common among traveling preachers. The "impure motives" could also refer to another trait such as greed or pride. Again, these were common among some traveling preachers. The believers knew that this accusation was not true, for they knew Paul and his companions.

Third, they were not using *trickery.* They had not tricked any of the believers into converting. They had not hidden any of the truth from those to whom they ministered. In this letter, Paul gave

CHARACTERISTICS OF A CHRISTIAN MINISTER

First Thessalonians 2 gives a rich description of how a true Christian minister (missionary, pastor, teacher) should look. Too often the bad examples are paraded in the media, while the many solid, Spirit-filled servants of God get little notice. Believers ought to be able to distinguish godly ministers from frauds, and Paul gave several ways to know.

Verse	A Godly Minister . . .
2:3	Speaks the truth and has pure motives in doing so.
2:4	Seeks to please God, not people.
2:5	Does not flatter; is not greedy.
2:6	Does not seek people's praise.
2:7	Is gentle, like a mother caring for her children.
2:8	Loves the believers and willingly shares his life and the gospel with them.
2:9	Works hard so as not to be a burden to anyone while preaching the Good News.
2:10	Is pure, honest, and faultless toward the believers.
2:11	Treats the believers as a good father would treat his own children.
2:12	Willingly pleads, encourages, and urges the believers to live in a way that God would consider worthy.

these believers deeper understanding of certain issues of the faith (such as the Resurrection and the Second Coming); he had not coerced people to believe by "tricking" them in any way.

To state this verse in its opposite, Paul was claiming, "You can see that we were preaching a message that is true, with motives that were pure, with methods that were completely honest."

SUFFERING FOR SHARING
Paul's claim that he had brought the gospel message to Thessalonica without trickery may have been a response to accusations from the Jewish leaders who had stirred up the crowds (Acts 17:5). Paul did not seek money, fame, or popularity by sharing the gospel. He demonstrated the sincerity of his motives by showing that he and Silas had suffered for sharing the gospel in Philippi. People become involved in ministry for a variety of reasons, not all of them good or pure. When their bad motives are exposed, all of Christ's work suffers. We should minister out of love for Christ and others with pure hearts and motives.

2:4 **For we speak as messengers approved by God to be entrusted with the Good News. Our purpose is to please God, not people. He alone examines the motives of our hearts.**NLT
Paul and his companions did not seek anything for themselves. Instead, they spoke only *as messengers approved by God to be entrusted with the Good News.* This was their commission; this was why they presented the Good News, faced persecution, and yet spoke the Good News some more. The verb "speak" *(laloumen)* is in the present tense, indicating that their speaking actively continued and would not be silenced by human beings. The word "approved" *(dokimasia)* means "tested." The word was used of testing a coin to see if it was genuine. Paul pictured himself and his companions as having been tested by God and shown to be trustworthy with the mission of telling the Good News.

These men had been approved because God had examined *the motives of [their] hearts* and had seen what he needed in these willing servants. No one can keep a secret from God. The "heart" refers to the "inner self"—the emotions, intellect, and will. When God examines the heart, he looks deeper than any human can look and understands the person completely. After looking deeply into Paul and Silas, God knew that these men had no desire to simply please people; instead, their *purpose [was] to please God.* Perhaps Paul had been accused of being a people pleaser because of the approach he had used to reach people (being all things to all people in order to win some; see 1 Corinthians 9:19-23). Paul's motive was never to advance his own cause or reputation, however, but to present the gospel for the good of the listener. See his words in Galatians 1:10 and Colossians 3:22.

Attempting to gain the approval of others will distract believers from pleasing God. As they do God's will, they must resist the desire to please people. The clarifying question of the believer should always be Who am I really serving? If the answer is "people," then the believer will be tossed back and forth by conflicting demands and expectations. But if the answer is consistently "Christ," the believer will have only one person to please and will not have to worry about how much or how little he or she is pleasing others. Paul wrote to the Colossians, "Then the way you live will always honor and please the Lord, and your lives will produce every kind of good fruit. All the while, you will grow as you learn to know God better and better" (Colossians 1:10 NLT). Seeking to serve Christ alone will settle many conflicts of interest!

GOSPEL TRUTH

Paul knew that he had been tested, approved, and trusted by God and that his goal was to please God. In trying to persuade people, some Christian leaders or workers may be tempted to alter their position or use flattery or praise just enough to make their message more palatable. Paul never changed his message to make it more acceptable, but he did tailor his methods to each audience. Although the presentation should be altered to be appropriate to the situation, the truth of the gospel must never be compromised. In your ministry, have you been tested by God, approved by God, and trusted by God? And are you seeking to please God? The vital ingredient of all successful ministry is the ability of the servant to put God directly at the center. Only then will he bless the minister's efforts.

2:5 **You know we never used flattery, nor did we put on a mask to cover up greed—God is our witness.**^{NIV} The accusers could say what they wished, but the believers in Thessalonica could attest to the fact that Paul and the others with him had *never used flattery.* "Flattery" means more than just saying nice words to someone. "Flattery," as used here, refers to using language in order to cajole someone—but always with a selfish motive. Paul had no selfish motives in preaching the gospel. He sought only to bring people to salvation in Christ.

The Thessalonians also knew that Paul and his fellow missionaries had not *put on a mask to cover up greed.* Many false teachers traveled about the ancient world willingly saying whatever an audience would pay to hear. Paul and Silas were not out to get money, nor were they greedy for fame or self-aggrandizement.

The Thessalonians knew these facts, but more important, *God* himself was a *witness* of Paul and Silas's motives and mission. And they were confident that God was pleased with their endeavors.

PHONIES

Paul avoided all forms of manipulation, especially flattery. It's disgusting to hear a person butter someone up. Flattery is phony, and it is a cover-up for a person's real intentions. Christians should not be flatterers. Those who proclaim God's truth have a special responsibility to be honest. Are you honest and straightforward in your words and actions? Or do you tell people what they want to hear in order to get what you want or to get ahead?

2:6 **As for human praise, we have never sought it from you or anyone else.**^{NLT} Paul and Silas had spoken only the truth in Thessalonica—no flattery to gain converts, no hidden motives to make something of themselves. They had not even desired *praise* from anyone. They didn't need people to compliment their hard work and eloquent speeches in order to feel that they had accomplished much. They didn't need anyone to praise them, for they sought approval from God alone.

WHO'S IMPRESSED?
When Paul was with the Thessalonians, he didn't flatter them, didn't seek their praise, and didn't become a burden to them. He and Silas focused their efforts completely on presenting God's message of salvation. This was important! The Thessalonian believers' lives were changed by God, not Paul; it was Christ's message they believed, not Paul's. When witnessing for Christ, our focus should not be on making a good impression. True ministers of Christ should point to him, not to themselves.

2:7 **As apostles of Christ we certainly had a right to make some demands of you, but instead we were like children among you. Or we were like a mother feeding and caring for her own children.**^{NLT} The *apostles* included the eleven men Jesus called (without Judas Iscariot), plus others, including Paul himself (Romans 1:1), Matthias (Acts 1:26), Barnabas (Acts 13:1-2; Galatians 2:9), Jesus' brother James (Galatians 1:19), Silas (1 Thessalonians 2:7), Andronicus, and Junia (Romans 16:7). Evidently the qualifications for being an apostle were to have seen the risen Christ, to have been commissioned by Christ to preach the gospel, and to be working on behalf of the kingdom, building its foundation. Paul also noted "signs and wonders and miracles" as marks of a true apostle (2 Corinthians 12:12 NLT). Only a few apostles brought the gospel message to the world.

As apostles, Paul and Silas *certainly had a right to make some demands* of the believers—such as expecting a certain amount of monetary help. In fact, most traveling teachers depended entirely on donations from their listeners. Paul practiced a trade (tent making) so as not to be a burden to his listeners (see also 2 Thessalonians 3:7-10). He also did not want to appear to be preaching for money. While he had a "right" to expect compensation (1 Corinthians 9:7-14), he did not always exercise that right. It was far more important to him that the gospel reach unbelievers, and he did not want anything to hinder it. In 1 Timothy 5:17-18, Paul establishes the right for ministers to receive remuneration: "The elders who direct the affairs of the church well are worthy of double honor, especially those whose work is preaching and teaching. For the Scripture says, 'Do not muzzle the ox while it is treading out the grain,' and 'The worker deserves his wages'" (NIV).

Instead of exercising their God-given authority as apostles, Paul and Silas *like children among* the Thessalonian believers, or *like a mother feeding and caring for her own children.* Some traveling teachers may have breezed into various towns with superior airs and high-minded attitudes. But this was not the case with God's missionaries. They had come with the authority of the God of heaven, yet they had served among the people with the kind gentleness of a loving and nurturing mother. Compare Paul's words in 2:11-12. Not only were they caring, they were protective as well. Paul expected the Thessalonians to treat each other this way too. For example, in his instructions at the end of this letter, he wrote, "Brothers and sisters, we urge you to warn those who are lazy. Encourage those who are timid. Take tender care of those who are weak. Be patient with everyone" (5:14 NLT).

GENTLE, GENTLE
Paul was caring as he ministered to the Thessalonian believers. Gentleness is often overlooked as a personal trait in our society. Power and assertiveness gain more respect, even though no one likes to be bullied. Gentleness means love in action—serving, being considerate, meeting the needs of others, allowing time for the other person to talk, and being willing to learn. It is an essential trait for both men and women. Maintain a gentle attitude in your relationships with others.

2:8 **We loved you so much that we were delighted to share with you not only the gospel of God but our lives as well, because you had become so dear to us.**[NIV] Paul and Silas cared for and nurtured the believers because they truly *loved* them. Far from being preachers who used their audiences for self-aggrandizement, Paul and Silas *were delighted to share* both *the gospel of God* and their *lives as well.* They joined with the Thessalonians in the day-to-day struggles and joys of life and were deeply involved with the people because those people *had become so dear* to them. Such sharing showed Paul and Silas's deep commitment to the gospel message and to the people with whom they shared it. Such care for the people could not be faked. The Thessalonian believers could attest to how much Paul and Silas loved them.

SHARING OUR LIVES
Paul not only shared the gospel, which many of us want to do,
but he shared his life as well. This involved sacrifice; looking out
for others' interests and not just his own (Philippians 2:17); and
close personal involvement, not impersonal clinical detachment.
He loved them—entering into their lives, their joys, and their
struggles.
    To be effective in reaching people, we must share ourselves
person-to-person. When a person feels cared for, he or she will
be open to listening to us share about our faith.

2:9 **You remember our labor and toil, brothers and sisters; we
worked night and day, so that we might not burden any
of you while we proclaimed to you the gospel of God.**^{NRSV}
Although Paul had the right to receive financial support from
the people he taught, he supported himself as a tent maker (Acts
18:3; 20:34; 1 Corinthians 4:12). Each Jewish boy would learn
a trade and try to earn his living with it. Paul had been trained
in tent making—cutting and sewing the woven cloth of goats'
hair into tents. Tents were used to house soldiers, so these tents
may have been sold to the Roman army. As a tent maker, Paul
was able to go wherever God led him, carrying his livelihood
with him. Paul modeled self-reliance, the opposite of those false
teachers and opportunists who sold religion in the marketplace.
Craftsmen in Paul's day worked sunrise to sunset. Paul's ministry
activities would have been at great sacrifice to him personally.
In Jewish tradition, rabbis were not to charge for their teaching
of the law but to earn their money in another trade or profession.
Paul didn't want to burden the young congregation by requiring
financial support. In the process of working at his trade, Paul and
Silas *proclaimed . . . the gospel of God.* The "double duty" of
earning a living while trying to preach, teach, and build up a body
of believers in Thessalonica called for exhausting *labor and toil*
as they worked *night and day.* But Paul and Silas gladly did it so
that they wouldn't be a *burden* to the new Thessalonian believers.

2:10 **You are witnesses, and so is God, of how holy, righteous and
blameless we were among you who believed.**^{NIV} Again Paul
appealed to what the Thessalonian believers knew about Paul and
Silas. The believers themselves were *witnesses* of how the missionaries had conducted themselves (see John 15:26-27; Acts 5:32).
Paul could not make these claims before the Thessalonians and
before *God* if the claims were not true. The accusing Jews could
say what they liked, but everyone knew that Paul and Silas had
conducted themselves in a *holy, righteous and blameless* manner.

The words should not be artificially separated by their meanings, for Paul probably was using words to describe conduct that was above reproach. Yet a study of the three words is helpful. The word "holy" *(hosios)* refers to being set apart by God, devoted to his service, and acting responsibly before him. "Righteous" *(dikaios)* focuses on obedience to God's law, coming up to his standard, being upright in dealings with people. "Blameless" *(amemptos)* points to their conduct toward the people, being without reproach. This consistent example of right living surely affected the Thessalonians. If Paul and Silas had shared the gospel message but had lived carelessly, their message would have had little impact. But they preached through both their words and their lives.

2:11-12 **For you know that we dealt with each of you as a father deals with his own children, encouraging, comforting and urging you to live lives worthy of God, who calls you into his kingdom and glory.**[NIV] Paul had already compared himself and Silas to a gentle and caring "mother" (2:7) in describing how they had brought the gospel message to the Thessalonians. The verses go on to describe Paul and Silas's role among the Thessalonians as being like a *father* in matters of teaching and raising these "baby believers." As a father *deals with his own children,* so the missionaries dealt with the new believers—each person, in fact, for the phrase "each of you" is emphatic. Paul and Silas had a personal relationship with each believer in Thessalonica.

First, Paul and Silas had been *encouraging* them. The Greek word for "encouraging" *(paraklesis)* means to come alongside with helpful instruction and insight (see also 4:18; 5:11). Second, they had been *comforting* them. "Comforting" *(paramytheomai)* is nearly synonymous and means to come alongside with sympathy and concern. This was especially important because terrible difficulties faced those who converted to Christianity. Third, they had been *urging* them *to live lives worthy of God.* "Urging" can refer to strong discipline applied appropriately as needed. It literally means "testifying." Paul did not water down the gospel message. All believers are given the task of conducting their daily activities *worthy of God* (see also Romans 16:2; Ephesians 4:1; Philippians 1:27; Colossians 1:10). To live "worthy of God" means to live consistently with his commands and character.

Paul had told the believers, and here he reminded them, that God alone *calls* them *into his kingdom and glory.* God's *kingdom* began when God himself entered human history as a man. Today Jesus Christ reigns in the hearts of believers, but the kingdom will not be fully realized until all evil in the world is judged and removed. Then God will reveal both his kingdom and his glory to those who have been "called" to join it. All who have accepted Christ as Savior have been called by God to be part of his family.

THE CARE OF YOUNG BELIEVERS
No loving father would neglect the safety of his children, allowing them to walk into circumstances that might be harmful or fatal. In the same way, we must take new believers under our wing until they are mature enough to stand firm in their faith. We must help new Christians become strong enough to influence others for the sake of the gospel. We can do this by helpful instruction and supporting encouragement. We must also warn them of pitfalls and temptations that they will face. Quite often they will need correction and rebuke. A good disciple, just like a good father, will not neglect to use discipline when needed.

2:13 **Therefore, we never stop thanking God that when you received his message from us, you didn't think of our words as mere human ideas. You accepted what we said as the very word of God—which, of course, it is. And this word continues to work in you who believe.**NLT Paul thanked God for how the Thessalonians had received the message. When Paul and Silas had preached, the people had recognized the *words* as being more than *human ideas*, and they had *accepted* the gospel message *as the very word of God.* The gospel message reveals its divine origin and power as it transforms people's lives. The Thessalonians were experiencing how *this word continues to work* in those *who believe.* Through his word, God works in believers' lives, transforming them, guiding them, cleansing them. Just as it was true for the Thessalonian believers, so it is true for all who believe—for those who accept the gospel message and trust in Christ as Savior. That message is still "the very word of God"— not one word has changed. It still transforms lives (Luke 8:11, 15; Hebrews 4:12).

2:14 **And then, dear brothers and sisters, you suffered persecution from your own countrymen. In this way, you imitated the believers in God's churches in Judea who, because of their belief in Christ Jesus, suffered from their own people, the Jews.**NLT The last statement of 2:13 points out that God's Word continues to work in believers. One evidence of this work was the Thessalonian believers' fortitude when they *suffered persecution from [their] own countrymen*—the Greeks in Thessalonica. But the believers in Thessalonica had good company, for in that persecution they had actually *imitated the believers in God's*

churches in Judea. Not that they had planned on this imitation—
but in the way they faced and withstood persecution, they were
just like the churches in Judea (see also 1:6 and commentary
there). While Acts 17:5-10 seems to indicate mostly Jewish opposition, it is certainly true that the Gentile Greeks were part of the
opposition because the Christians refused to participate in the
imperial religion.

WORDS AT WORK
Paul said that the word of God continued to work in the believers' lives. Paul knew that God's words are not mere sermons
or documents but a real source of transforming power. In Galatians 1:11-12, Paul said that the "gospel message I preach is
not based on mere human reasoning. . . . I received it by direct
revelation from Jesus Christ" (NLT). It is not magical in the sense
that we can leave a Bible verse for someone and expect that he
or she will become a Christian instantly. But those who read the
Bible and study Christ's life in the Gospels can still be convinced
of their need for salvation. Encourage your non-Christian friends
to read God's Word. It works wonders.

The Christians in Judea suffered *because of their belief in
Christ Jesus,* and they *suffered from their own people, the Jews.*
It had been persecution in Judea that had driven the believers out
of that country to various places—and the gospel went with them.
The book of Acts relates some of the early persecution that was
going on in Jerusalem and Judea. This suffering is described in
the following verses. When Paul referred to the "Jews" causing
all kinds of persecution, he was speaking of specific Jews who
were opposing his preaching of the gospel. He did not mean all
Jews. Many of Paul's converts were Jewish, and Paul himself was
a Jew (2 Corinthians 11:22).

2:15-16 **For some of the Jews killed the prophets, and some even
killed the Lord Jesus. Now they have persecuted us, too. They
fail to please God and work against all humanity as they try
to keep us from preaching the Good News of salvation to the
Gentiles. By doing this, they continue to pile up their sins. But
the anger of God has caught up with them at last.**NLT Paul's
most recent relationship with the Jews had been when he was
persecuted in Philippi (Acts 16:22-24) and driven out of Thessalonica (Acts 17:5-6, 10). In Corinth, from which he was writing
this letter to Thessalonica, he had been so insulted by the Jews
that he said, "From now on I will go preach to the Gentiles" (Acts
18:6 NLT).

Persecution did not surprise Paul, for Jesus himself had warned that his followers would face just such animosity (John 15:18). The churches had grown to expect persecution from both hostile Jews and Gentiles. Paul would later write to Timothy, "Everyone who wants to live a godly life in Christ Jesus will suffer persecution" (2 Timothy 3:12 NLT).

Why were the Jews so hostile to Christianity? The Jewish people had a history of killing *the prophets.* Jesus had said to the Jewish leaders of his day—speaking of the past and predicting what they would do to his followers:

> *Woe to you, teachers of the law and Pharisees! . . . You testify against yourselves that you are the descendants of those who murdered the prophets. . . . Therefore I am sending you prophets and wise men and teachers. Some of them you will kill and crucify; others you will flog in your synagogues and pursue from town to town. And so upon you will come all the righteous blood that has been shed on earth, from the blood of righteous Abel to the blood of Zechariah son of Berekiah, whom you murdered between the temple and the altar. . . . O Jerusalem, Jerusalem, you who kill the prophets and stone those sent to you, how often I have longed to gather your children together, as a hen gathers her chicks under her wings, but you were not willing.* (Matthew 23:29, 31, 34-35, 37 NIV)

This is a brief history of Old Testament martyrdom. Abel was the first martyr (Genesis 4); Zechariah is the last mentioned in the Hebrew Bible, which ended with 2 Chronicles. Zechariah is a classic example of a man of God who was killed by those who claimed to be God's people (see 2 Chronicles 24:20-21).

Despite the Jews' constant watching for the arrival of their promised Messiah, they missed him when he came, and *even killed* him (see Matthew 27:25). The Jewish leaders thought Jesus was a false prophet, and they didn't want his teachings to spread, so they opposed all who preached about him (Acts 4:18).

The Jewish opposition to Christianity continued after Jesus' death. Although the Jewish religion had been declared legal by the Roman government, it still had a tenuous relationship with the government. At this time, Christianity was viewed as a sect of Judaism. The Jews were afraid that reprisals leveled against the Christians might be expanded to include them. In addition, the Jewish leaders feared that if many Jews were drawn away into Christianity, their own political position might be weakened. The leaders were also proud of their special status as God's chosen people, and they resented the fact that the Christians were *preaching the Good News . . . to the Gentiles* and including Gentile

believers as full members in the church. The Jews' natural animosity against Gentiles extended to trying to hinder their *salvation.* As the people who should have recognized the Messiah and
welcomed all who would come to the one true God, the Jewish
leaders failed miserably and actually feared that others might find
salvation.

By doing this, Paul wrote, *they continue to pile up their sins.*
This opposition to God was another in a long series of rebellions
that was building up their guilt for the time when God's punishment would be revealed. The inevitable consequence of this
attitude would be *the anger of God* (for more on God's wrath, see
1:7-10 and commentary there). There are several interpretations
of the words "has caught up with them at last":

- Writing this letter in A.D. 50, Paul may have been referring to
  the severe famine in Judea in A.D. 45–47 (Acts 11:27-28), the
  massacre of Jews in the temple area in A.D. 49 (recorded by
  Josephus), or the expulsion of Jews from Rome by Emperor
  Claudius (Acts 18:2).
- Paul may have been foreseeing disastrous coming events, such
  as the destruction of Jerusalem in A.D. 70. The Jews' continued
  rejection of the gospel message would spell destruction.
- Most likely, Paul was using language conveying the "dramatic
  present." He was talking about the future as though it had
  already happened in order to make a point. Because of their
  continual rejection of Jesus as the Messiah and the believers as
  his followers, the Jews were not only piling up their guilt but
  were hardening their hearts to the point of no return.

These surely were difficult words for Paul, a Jew from birth,
to write about his countrymen. In another letter Paul wrote, "The
longing of my heart and my prayer to God is for the people of
Israel to be saved" (Romans 10:1 NLT). Paul understood that the
Jews were God's chosen people and that many of them *would*
come to salvation in Christ. He also knew, however, that many
would flatly reject the truth (Romans 11 explains this). This
pained him greatly. Especially when those Jews were attacking
him outright.

2:17   **Dear brothers and sisters, after we were separated from you
for a little while (though our hearts never left you), we tried
very hard to come back because of our intense longing to see
you again.**[NLT] The accusers had attacked Paul and Silas's methods and message (Paul refuted the accusations in the previous
verses). The accusers also had pointed out the sudden departure
of the missionaries and the fact that they had not soon returned,

implying that Paul and Silas had lied and were too scared to
return. So Paul explained that the separation had not been desired
(they did not separate themselves but *were separated from* the
Thessalonians). The word "separated" is also translated "torn
away." In addition, while physically separated, the missionaries kept the believers in their hearts. They had *tried very hard to
come back* and had an *intense longing* to be back in Thessalonica
with the believers. The next verse explains why.

2:18 **For we wanted to come to you—certainly I, Paul, wanted to
again and again—but Satan blocked our way.**[NRSV] Far from
being afraid to return, Paul and Silas *wanted to* go back to Thessalonica. Paul's inclusion of his personal emphasis—*certainly I,
Paul, wanted to again and again*—simply gave credence to what
he has written in 2:17.

PRAYER WARFARE
During his time under house arrest. Paul saw many Roman
soldiers up close—their polished armor, full-length shields, and
glistening swords. In Ephesians 6, Paul used the armor of a
Roman soldier to illustrate the Christian's resources when facing
the realities of spiritual warfare. Christians belong to a spiritual
army, which is battling Satan and all his wicked allies. The most
effective strategy against this evil opponent is prayer based on
the Word of God. Prayer for Christians throughout the world can
make a dramatic difference in their lives—physical needs can be
miraculously met; despondent souls can be suddenly refreshed.
Prayer for courageous missionaries will ensure that God's message will be heard around the world. The parents of Hudson
Taylor, missionary to China, believed that their prayers would
affect the lives of the Chinese, and they did. Don't cultivate a
lazy habit of prayer. Be alert. Be persistent in your prayers. The
eternal destiny of souls throughout the world is at stake.

Yet they could not because *Satan blocked* them. Satan is real.
He is called "the god of this age" (2 Corinthians 4:4 NIV) and
"the ruler of the kingdom of the air" (Ephesians 2:2 NIV). What
exactly blocked Paul and Silas from returning to Thessalonica—
opposition, illness, travel complications, or a direct attack by
Satan—is unknown. But somehow Satan had been able to keep
them away more than once (Paul had wanted *again and again* to
return, but each time had been prevented). The word "blocked"
(enekophein) means "to cut into or break up," as destroying a
road or a bridge, or to block the progress of an army. The Thessalonian believers must have known what Paul was talking about,
so Paul gave no further details.
Spiritual warfare exists. Satan and God are constantly at war.

Satan actively works to keep people from accepting Christ. He also works to hinder God's people from doing kingdom work. Some of the difficulties that prevent believers from accomplishing God's work can be attributed to Satan (see Ephesians 6:12). Satan will bring sexual temptation on those who lack self-control (1 Corinthians 7:5). He will bring in false teaching to lead believers astray (2 Corinthians 11:3). Satan can even disguise himself as an "angel of light" (2 Corinthians 11:14 NLT). Satan will also attempt to hurt the community of believers through persecution (1 Thessalonians 3:1-5). While God is more powerful than Satan and sometimes intervenes and overrides, he does not always do so. Therefore, Christians must be vigilant and faithful to Christ.

2:19-20 **For what is our hope, our joy, or the crown in which we will glory in the presence of our Lord Jesus when he comes? Is it not you? Indeed, you are our glory and joy.**[NIV] With overflowing love for this young church, Paul asked a question and then answered it himself. What was the *hope, . . . joy, or . . . crown in which* Paul and Silas would be able to *glory in the presence of [the] Lord Jesus when he comes?* It would be the Thessalonian believers! The word "hope" describes Paul's confidence in these believers. The word "joy" pictures his own inner feelings when he will see them presented to the Lord and welcomed into the kingdom. The "crown" pictures a victor's wreath—the believers were like a victory crown, giving Paul joy in having "run the race" for their sakes (1 Corinthians 9:25; Philippians 4:1). One day we all will stand together before the Lord Jesus at his second coming. Paul imagined how he would rejoice with the believers who had come to faith through his preaching. The words "glory and joy" could refer to both outward and inward feelings. In these words, Paul left no question about how he felt toward these new believers. His love for them welled over into praise to God and joy in partnering with God for bringing them the message of eternal life.

ULTIMATE REWARDS
The ultimate reward for Paul's ministry was not money, prestige, or fame but new believers whose lives had been changed by God through the preaching of the gospel. This was why he longed to see them. No matter what ministry God has given to you, your highest reward and greatest joy should be those who come to believe in Christ and are growing in him.

---

1 Thessalonians 3

Chapter 3 continues the concerns of chapter 2. Paul had been
explaining to the Thessalonian believers why he and Silas had
been unable to return to them. It had not been, as their detractors
had said, because of fear or because they had been lying. Instead,
Paul and Silas had wanted to come back but had been prevented
by evil spiritual forces (2:18). They did not leave the young
believers in Thessalonica without help, however, as the following
verses explain.

**3:1-3 Finally, when we could stand it no longer, we decided to stay
alone in Athens, and we sent Timothy to visit you. He is our
brother and God's co-worker in proclaiming the Good News
of Christ.**NLT Because Paul could not return to Thessalonica
(2:18), he sent Timothy as his representative. According to Acts
17:10, Paul left Thessalonica and went to Berea. When trouble
broke out in Berea, some Christians took Paul to Athens, while
Silas and Timothy stayed behind (Acts 17:13-15). Then Paul
directed Silas and Timothy to join him in Athens. Later, Paul sent
Timothy to encourage the Thessalonian Christians to be strong in
their faith in the face of persecution and other troubles.

Paul's inability to return to Thessalonica and support the
new church weighed heavily upon him. All three of the letter's
senders—Paul, Silas, and Timothy (1:1)—*could stand it no longer.* Communication was very slow in ancient times. Therefore,
when no communication arrived from the church, the missionaries had no idea what was happening to these young believers.
The Jews had chased the missionaries out of the city, so it was
fair to assume that the new Christians were under attack as well.
Concern for the believers caused Paul and his companions to
take action. They decided that Paul and Silas would stay in Athens while they sent Timothy back to Thessalonica to visit the
believers. The word "alone" is plural in Greek—"we should stay
here ourselves." Paul and Silas stayed behind and sent Timothy.
The word "alone" also expresses a sense of desolation, of being

left behind. This was a difficult decision. Paul really wanted to go back himself; because he could not go, however, at least his *co-worker* could go in his place. The word for "co-worker" is *synergos*. It is one of nine different terms that Paul used for his partners in ministry. In Acts and other letters, over one hundred individuals have been identified as "co-workers." Some of the terms (taken from the NLT) used include

"Brother" . . . Apollos . . . 1 Corinthians 16:12
"Apostle" . . . Silas . . . 1 Thessalonians 2:7
"Assistant" . . . Erastus . . . Acts 19:22
"Co-worker" . . . Urbanus . . . Romans 16:9
"Partner" . . . Philemon . . . Philemon 1:17
"Work[er]" . . . Mary . . . Romans 16:6
"Good soldier" . . . Timothy . . . 2 Timothy 2:3
"Fellow prisoner" . . . Epaphras . . . Philemon 1:23
"True partner" . . . Syzygus . . . Philippians 4:3

ADVENTURE HIGHLIGHTS FROM TIMOTHY'S LIFE
Before beginning his travels, Timothy submitted to being circumcised by Paul. Paul felt this was important "because of the Jews who were in those places [where Timothy lived], for they all knew that his father was a Greek" (Acts 16:3 NRSV).

When Paul escaped to Athens from the upheaval in Berea, Silas and Timothy remained behind, undoubtedly to continue to teach (Acts 17:10-15). Silas and Timothy later rejoined Paul in Corinth (Acts 18:1, 5). Timothy was in Corinth with Paul when Paul wrote his letter to the Romans (Romans 16:21).

Later Paul remained in Ephesus but sent Timothy and Erastus (another assistant) on ahead into Macedonia (Acts 19:22).

Paul sent Timothy to Corinth (1 Corinthians 4:17; 16:10), and Timothy was with Paul when Paul wrote 2 Corinthians (2 Corinthians 1:1, 19).

Paul sent Timothy to Thessalonica (1 Thessalonians 3:2); Timothy was also with Paul when Paul wrote to that church in response to the good news that Timothy had brought regarding the Thessalonians' faith (1 Thessalonians 1:1; 3:6).

Timothy was with Paul when Paul wrote to the church in Philippi, and Timothy went as Paul's emissary to that church (Philippians 1:1; 2:19).

Timothy was with Paul when Paul wrote his letters to the Colossians and to Philemon (Colossians 1:1; Philemon 1:1).

Timothy had grown up in Lystra, a city in the province of Galatia. Paul and Barnabas had visited Lystra on Paul's first missionary journey (see Acts 14:8-21). Most likely, Paul had met the young Timothy and his mother, Eunice, and grandmother Lois (see 2 Timothy 1:5) on this journey, perhaps even staying in their home.

On Paul's second missionary journey, he and Silas went to several cities that Paul had already visited, including Lystra, "where there was a disciple named Timothy, the son of a Jewish woman who was a believer. . . . He was well spoken of by the believers in Lystra and Iconium. Paul wanted Timothy to accompany him" (Acts 16:1-3 NRSV). So began a great adventure for this young *brother* in the faith, Timothy, who would travel the empire with Paul, *proclaiming the Good News of Christ.* He became Paul's assistant—traveling with him and sometimes for him, as Paul's emissary (see box), as here in his return to Thessalonica.

We sent him to strengthen you, to encourage you in your faith, and to keep you from being shaken by the troubles you were going through. But you know that we are destined for such troubles.NLT Timothy had three main tasks for his return to Thessalonica—*to strengthen* the believers, *to encourage* them, and *to keep [them] from being shaken by . . . troubles.* In addition, Paul wanted him to "find out about [their] faith" (3:5 NIV). Paul was concerned that the opposition had caused disruption in the church, so he wanted Timothy to find out how their faith was holding up against persecution. To "strengthen" them meant that Timothy would teach them and build them up in their Christian walk. The word translated "encourage" is *parakaleo,* to comfort or exhort (see 2:12; 4:18).

Paul had been convinced of the genuine conversion experience of these believers (1:5), but he also knew the importance of follow-up and discipleship. Faith needs to be strengthened and encouraged, so Timothy went back to do just that for these believers. Paul also knew that facing "troubles" because of one's faith in Christ should be expected. Inevitably, tribulations would come from a society opposed to the values at the core of Christianity (Mark 8:34; John 16:33; Acts 14:22). Paul wanted the believers in Thessalonica to know that the "troubles" they *were going through* were not unusual. Instead, they were even to be expected, for Christians *are destined for such troubles.* The word "destined" is *keimetha* and conveys that God appoints those who stand for him, and, as a result, they experience persecution by society (2 Thessalonians 1:4-10). The concept refers to the inevitability of opposition rather than God's predetermined will that people suffer. Suffering comes with the territory. The Thessalonians were suffering (1:6), and though they had held strong, Paul wanted to make sure they understood that suffering should be expected. See John 15:18–16:4 for Christ's teaching on the inevitability of persecution for believers.

THE TOUGH TIMES
Paul encouraged the Thessalonians as they faced persecution. Some think that troubles are always caused by sin or a lack of faith. But trials may be part of God's plan for believers. Experiencing problems and persecution can build character (James 1:2-4), perseverance (Romans 5:3-5), and sensitivity toward others who also face trouble (2 Corinthians 1:3-7). Problems are inevitable for God's people. Your troubles may be a sign of effective Christian living. Some people turn to God with the hope of escaping suffering on earth. But God doesn't promise that. Instead he gives us power to grow through our sufferings. The Christian life involves obedience to Christ despite opposition and hardship. Therefore, we must not resent it when trouble comes but trust God for strength to remain faithful to him.

3:4 **In fact, when we were with you, we kept telling you that we would be persecuted. And it turned out that way, as you well know.**[NIV] Paul's preaching to new converts regularly included the reality of persecution. He never taught that Christ would make life easy. He had constantly faced persecution for his faith, and he explained that any of his converts would do likewise. The Thessalonians could attest to this fact—for Paul and Silas had *kept telling* them that they *would be persecuted.* Paul had said that persecution would occur in Thessalonica—*and it turned out that way,* as the believers well knew. The missionaries had been run out of town for preaching the Good News (Acts 17:5-10).

REAL VICTORY
Paul predicted continued persecution, which had been the common experience of Jesus and the disciples. Jesus sacrificed his physical life, and many of the disciples suffered for the faith—even dying for it. Real discipleship implies real commitment—we must pledge everything to his service. Those who spend their whole lives trying to avoid danger, pain, or discomfort may isolate themselves from being able to contribute or serve at all. If our aim is only to protect ourselves from criticism and hardship, we begin to die spiritually and emotionally. Our lives turn inward, and we lose our intended purpose. When we serve Christ, the trials we face help us grow.

3:5 **For this reason, when I could stand it no longer, I sent to find out about your faith. I was afraid that in some way**

**the tempter might have tempted you and our efforts might
have been useless.**^{NIV} *For this reason*—because persecution had
occurred against the missionaries—Paul *could stand . . . no longer* the suspense of not knowing how the believers were getting
along. So Paul *sent to find out about [their] faith* by sending Timothy (3:2) to find out if their faith was holding up to persecution
and if they were persevering in the face of difficulty. The words
"I was afraid" could also simply mean "lest" (as in the NKJV).
The focus is not so much on fear as on concern that *in some way
the tempter might have tempted [them].* Paul was concerned
that the new and struggling believers might turn away from their
faith. Satan ("the tempter") is the most powerful of the evil spirits
(2:18). His power can affect both the spiritual world (Ephesians
2:1-3; 6:10-12) and the physical world (Job 1–2). Satan is an
angel who rebelled against God. He is real, not symbolic, and is
constantly working against God and those who obey him. Satan
tempted Eve in the Garden and persuaded her to sin; he tempted
Jesus in the desert and did not persuade him to fall (Matthew
4:1-11). To be tempted is not a sin. Tempting others or giving in
to temptation is sin.

THE TEMPTER
Paul warned against Satan, "the tempter." Satan and his forces
are aggressive. We face a powerful army whose goal is to
defeat Christ's church. When we believe in Christ, these beings
become our enemies, and they try every device to turn us away
from him and back to sin. Although we are assured of victory,
we must engage in the struggle until Christ returns because
Satan is constantly battling against all who are on the Lord's
side. We need supernatural power to defeat Satan, and God has
provided this by giving us his Holy Spirit within us and his armor
surrounding us. If you feel discouraged, remember Jesus' words
to Peter: "Now I say to you that you are Peter (which means
'rock'), and upon this rock I will build my church, and all the
powers of hell will not conquer it" (Matthew16:18 NLT).

3:6 **But Timothy has just now come to us from you, and has
brought us the good news of your faith and love. He has told
us also that you always remember us kindly and long to see
us—just as we long to see you.**^{NRSV} Timothy had been sent to
nurture the believers and also to find out how they were doing
so as to report back to Paul. At the writing of this letter, Timothy
had just returned and *brought . . . good news of* the Thessalonian
believers' *faith and love.* The word translated "brought good
news" is *euangelizomai,* used elsewhere in the New Testament

only of bringing the gospel, the Good News. That Paul used it
here describes how he felt when Timothy came back with "good
news" about the Thessalonian church. Their faith was solid, their
love strong, and they remembered Paul and Silas *kindly,* longing
to see them. What relief Paul must have felt! Far from having
been beleaguered by the opposition and turned against the faith,
the believers had stayed strong; they even longed to see Paul and
Silas as much as Paul and Silas longed to see them.

WE LONG TO SEE YOU
The Thessalonians longed to see Paul. Have you ever longed
to see a friend with whom you share fond memories? Paul had
such a longing to see the Christians at Thessalonica. His love
and affection for them was based not merely upon past experi-
ences but also upon the unity that comes when believers draw
upon Christ's love. All Christians are part of God's family and
thus share in the transforming power of his love. Do you feel
a deep love for fellow Christians, friends and strangers alike?
Let Christ's love motivate you to love other Christians and to
express that love in your actions toward them.

3:7-8 **So we have been greatly encouraged in the midst of our**
troubles and suffering, dear brothers and sisters, because
you have remained strong in your faith. It gives us new life to
know that you are standing firm in the Lord.^{NLT} Paul's certain
relief and joy at the good news from Thessalonica was matched
by great comfort that they had *remained strong* in the faith. Paul
and Silas had continued to experience *troubles and suffering,* but
this report from Timothy encouraged and inspired them with *new*
life—renewed energy and vigor (see also 4:18; 5:11; Romans
1:12). Their efforts in Thessalonica had not been useless (3:5).
The believers were *standing firm in the Lord,* and that was
a great reward. Believers' lives are bound up with one another.
It should bring great joy to a believer's heart when he or she hears
that another believer is standing firm in the faith despite
difficulties.

3:9-10 **How we thank God for you! Because of you we have great joy**
as we enter God's presence. Night and day we pray earnestly
for you, asking God to let us see you again to fill the gaps in
your faith.^{NLT} It brings *great joy* to a Christian to see another
person come to faith in Christ and mature in that faith. Paul experienced this joy countless times. He thanked God for those in
Thessalonica who had come to know Christ and had held strong
in the faith. Paul had been forced to leave while they were still

immature believers with incomplete knowledge. Yet they had held on to their faith despite opposition and persecution and had come through unscathed. No wonder Paul thanked God!

Entering "God's presence" refers to the context of prayer. Paul also *earnestly* prayed, *night and day,* or constantly, for their continued growth. He also asked God to let him and his co-workers return to Thessalonica. Thus far, Satan had hindered them, but Satan's hindrances only happen with God's permission. So Paul asked God to allow them to go back *to fill the gaps in [their] faith.* Paul wanted to give them further teaching, move on to deeper doctrines, and help these believers mature in Christ. He would not be dealing with lack of faith or any fatal flaw of heresy. Rather, his interest was to help the believers reach maturity (Ephesians 4:12-13). He wanted to fill up any deficiencies and foster continued growth. (See the commentary on Colossians 1:24, pages 166–171, in *Life Application Bible Commentary: Philippians, Colossians & Philemon.*)

> From this also it appears how necessary it is for us to give careful attention to doctrine, for teachers were not appointed merely with the view of leading men, in the course of a single day or month, to the faith of Christ, but for the purpose of perfecting the faith which has been begun.   *John Calvin*

MUTUAL BENEFITS
Because the believers had been faithful, Paul's life had been renewed and revived. Have you benefited from the ministry of others? Has a pastor, youth worker, or Sunday school teacher's guidance and faithfulness stimulated you to grow in Christ? Consider how you may bring some word of encouragement or some thoughtful gift. Let that important person know that you have followed his or her example by being faithful to Christ.

3:11 Now may our God and Father himself and our Lord Jesus clear the way for us to come to you.[NIV] The first half of the letter closes with Paul's praying that he might enjoy a reunion with the Christians in Thessalonica. Paul made it clear in this letter that he really wanted to return to Thessalonica (2:17-18; 3:6, 10). He repeated his desire, breaking into prayer here, calling upon *our God and Father himself and our Lord Jesus* to *clear the way* for them to return.

It is unclear whether Paul ever returned to Thessalonica, but he traveled through Asia on his third journey and was joined by Aristarchus and Secundus, who were from Thessalonica (Acts 20:4-5).

3:12 And may the Lord make you increase and abound in love for one another and for all, just as we abound in love for you.NRSV Paul wanted to return, and he prayed to do so (3:11). No matter what happened, however, Paul knew that the church needed to sustain itself. A key ingredient would be *love* among the believers—as opposed to disunity, factions, or disagreements. The church would need love to survive. Although Paul had received good news from Timothy of the Thessalonians' love (3:6), he knew that love can always be strengthened and deepened with God's help. So Paul prayed that *the Lord* would make the believers *increase and abound in love for one another,* and not just one another but *for all.* The word for "love," *agape,* describes the selfless love that comes from God. Such love looks out for the best interests of those loved—caring for fellow believers and reaching out to unbelievers. Such love can withstand much difficulty. Paul and his companions already "abounded" in this love for the Thessalonians, as seen in their willingness to face persecution to bring the Thessalonians the Good News.

INCREASE AND ABOUND
Paul prayed for the Thessalonians' love to increase. If we are full of God's love, it will overflow to others. It's not enough merely to be courteous to others; we must actively and persistently show love to them. Our love should be growing continually. If your capacity to love has remained unchanged for some time, ask God to fill you again from his never-ending supply. Then look for opportunities to express his love.

3:13 May he strengthen your hearts so that you will be blameless and holy in the presence of our God and Father when our Lord Jesus comes with all his holy ones.NIV That God would "strengthen [their] hearts" refers to Paul's desire for the Thessalonians to continue to have inner strength. In Scripture, the "heart" refers to the inner sphere of emotion, desire, and will—the personality. Such strength would be seen in one's character—and so Paul prayed that they would *be blameless and holy.* Complete perfection is not attainable in this life, but the process of sanctification brings believers ever closer to perfection. One day, the process will be over, and all believers will be made perfect *in the presence of our God and Father.* The phrase "when our Lord Jesus comes with all his holy ones" refers to the second coming

of Christ, when he will establish his eternal kingdom. There
are two views about the identity of these *holy ones.* Some think
it refers to believers; others say it refers to angels. Most likely
both are true because the words "holy ones" have been used to
describe angels as well as believers. Because Paul used the inclu-
sive word "all" to describe this group, it seems that those who
come with Christ at his second coming will be the angels and
the believers who have died (see Matthew 13:41; 25:31; Mark
8:38; 13:27; Luke 9:26; 2 Thessalonians 1:7). At that time Christ
will gather all believers, those who have died and those who are
alive, into one united family under his rule. All believers from all
times, including these Thessalonians, will be with Christ in his
kingdom.

1 Thessalonians 4

LIVE TO PLEASE GOD / 4:1-12

The first three chapters of this letter focus on looking back at Paul's visit with the Thessalonians and defending his ministry with them against his critics. The final two chapters look ahead to the future of the church—giving advice for certain areas of Christian conduct that he felt needed to be addressed. The end of chapter 3 is a prayer that Christ would make these believers strong, blameless, and holy before God (3:13). That is a process of walking in faith and learning to live to please God. Effective faith should show itself in every area of a believer's life.

4:1-2 Finally, brothers and sisters, we ask and urge you in the Lord Jesus that, as you learned from us how you ought to live and to please God (as, in fact, you are doing), you should do so more and more. For you know what instructions we gave you through the Lord Jesus.NRSV The word "finally" signals a change in subject as Paul moved on to practical application of faith. Apparently Timothy's report (3:6) had brought Paul great joy regarding the believers' faith but also included a few noteworthy concerns, for Paul here gave instructions for right living in some very specific situations.

The believers had learned from Paul and his companions *how [they] ought to live and to please God* (2:4-12). The missionaries had set an example for them of Christlike living. Evidently they had learned, for Paul said that they were *doing* just that, but he wanted them to *do so more and more.* They already knew *what instructions* Paul and Silas had given them *through the Lord Jesus.* These instructions were not Paul's made-up desires for them to follow him; rather, these instructions in right living came "through the Lord Jesus himself." They are important for every believer of every generation. Living to please God is every Christian's priority. Knowing Jesus as Savior brings salvation and should lead every believer to want to live to please him in gratefulness for what he has done. Through obedient believers, God works in the world. Obedience pleases God. People cannot claim to know and love God if they do not seek to please him.

PLEASING GOD
How do we please God? (Verses quoted from NIV, italics added.)

- Genesis 8:21: "The LORD smelled the *pleasing* aroma" of the sacrifice. In the Old Testament, God's pleasure in the aroma of a sacrifice meant that he had accepted the sacrifice for sin. Thus, pleasing God means making an acceptable sacrifice to him.
- Psalm 19:14: "May the words of my mouth and the meditation of my heart be *pleasing* in your sight." Our love for God should guide what we think and what we say (see also Psalm 104:34).
- John 5:30: "I seek not to *please* myself but him who sent me." Jesus taught us not to try to please ourselves but to please God (see also John 8:29).
- Romans 12:1: "Offer your bodies as living sacrifices, holy and *pleasing* to God." God wants us to turn over our lives to him daily, renouncing our own desires and trusting him to guide us (see also Romans 14:8-18).
- Ephesians 5:10: "Find out what *pleases* the Lord." We must live in contrast to those who live immorally.
- Colossians 1:10: "We pray this in order that you may live a life worthy of the Lord and may *please* him in every way: bearing fruit in every good work, growing in the knowledge of God." Bearing fruit and growing in the knowledge of God are ways to please him.
- Hebrews 11:6: "Without faith it is impossible to *please* God." God rewards with his presence those who trust him fully.

4:3-5 **God's will is for you to be holy, so stay away from all sexual sin. Then each of you will control his own body and live in holiness and honor—not in lustful passion like the pagans who do not know God and his ways.**[NLT] The phrase "God's will is for you to be holy" is also translated, "It is God's will that you should be sanctified" (NIV). Becoming "holy" involves a process called "sanctification." This process continues throughout every believer's lifetime on earth, preparing him or her for heaven. God takes the old patterns and behaviors and transforms them to his standards and will. Those who are being sanctified have accepted Christ as Savior and are allowing the Holy Spirit to work in their lives, making them more and more like Christ.

> If the heathen behave as they do because they do not know God, Christians must behave in a completely different way because we do know God, because he is a holy God, because he is our God, and because we want to please him.
> *John Stott*

Because God wants his people to become holy, believers need to uphold certain standards here on earth. Christianity is not a list of dos and don'ts but a relationship in which believers desire to please their heavenly Father (2:4; 4:1). To please him requires obedience to *his* standards. Apparently the area of *sexual sin* (Greek, *porneia*) was plaguing the church in Thessalonica, as it was plaguing the Roman Empire as a whole. The many idols worshiped in the regions across the empire often had an emphasis on sex—some temples even employed prostitutes for the pleasure of "worshipers." In general, people regarded any kind of sexual activity as acceptable. It was quite common for a man *not* to limit his sexual relationship to his wife. Homosexuality was common. Incest was overlooked. Slaves were kept and used for sex.

God's standards are the opposite. Paul taught abstinence from sexual immorality. This included any kind of illegitimate sexual intercourse or relationship outside of marriage. He forbade any homosexual activity. In Corinth some of the new Christians had been prostitutes, adulterers, or homosexuals. When they came to Christ out of such perversion, they had to alter their attitude toward this particular area of life. They had to accept God's standards—which had to be taught to them, as Paul was teaching them here.

We live in a society similar to the one in which Paul lived and taught. Every kind of sexual activity, including violence and abuse of children, has become commonplace. Unbridled expression of all desires has become the norm. As Christians, we must uphold the sanctity of sexual expression within the loving commitment of the marriage relationship.

NEVER UNDERESTIMATE

Sexual immorality is a temptation that is always before us. Movies and TV shows present sex outside marriage as a normal, even desirable, part of life, while marriage is often pictured as confining and joyless. Those who are pure are often mocked. God does not forbid sexual sin just to be difficult. He knows its power to destroy us physically and spiritually. No one should underestimate the power of sexual immorality. It has devastated countless lives and destroyed families, churches, communities, and even nations.

Sexual desires and activities must be placed under Christ's control. God created sex for procreation and pleasure and as an expression of love between a husband and wife. Sexual experience must be limited to the marriage relationship to avoid hurting ourselves, our relationship to God, and our relationships with others. God wants to protect us from damaging ourselves and others, so he offers to fill us—our loneliness, our desires—with himself.

These believers were not being exhorted to *stay away from* (literally, "abstain from") all sex but from all sexual sin. God created sex to be a beautiful and essential ingredient of marriage, but sex outside the marriage relationship is sin. That is where God drew the line. These believers had to *stay away from* all forms of sexual sin—keep clear of or even run away if need be (see also 1 Corinthians 6:13-20; 2 Corinthians 12:21). Therefore, Paul taught that believers must *control* their bodies *and live in holiness and honor—not in lustful passion like the pagans who do not know God and his ways.* Sex should be kept within the context of marriage between a man and woman; sex should be done in "holiness and honor—not in lustful passion." Honorable conduct is contrasted with an evil, lustful attitude that can contaminate even a marriage. People who live by "lustful passion" are ignorant of God because they have chosen to ignore the knowledge of him that they have been given (Romans 1:19-20, 24-27) and to ignore his messengers who bring the Good News to them.

PASSIONS
Paul said that lustful passions should not control God's people. Some argue that if they've already sinned by having lustful thoughts, they might as well go ahead with lustful actions too. Acting out sinful desires is harmful in several ways: (1) It causes people to excuse sin rather than to stop sinning; (2) it destroys marriages; (3) it is deliberate rebellion against God's Word; and (4) it always hurts someone else in addition to the sinner. Sinful action is more dangerous than sinful desire, so desires should not be acted out. Nevertheless, sinful desire is just as damaging to righteousness. Left unchecked, wrong desires will result in wrong actions and will turn people away from God.

4:6 And that in this matter no one should wrong his brother or take advantage of him. The Lord will punish men for all such sins, as we have already told you and warned you.NIV These words "in this matter" refer to what Paul had just written regarding sexual sin (4:3). Paul focused here on the men among the believers. Not only does sexual sin ruin the holy and honorable living to which Christian men should aspire, but it also is a sin against one's fellowmen—whether they are Christians or not. To have a sexual affair with another man's wife or member of his household wrongs that other man. It takes advantage of a trusting relationship. To have premarital sex, or a sexual affair with a woman who is unmarried, also wrongs another man, for the woman cannot bring virginity to her marriage. God does not overlook these sins; instead, he *will punish men for all such sins.* So important was this that Paul and Silas had *already told* and *warned* the new Christians in Thessalonica. While Paul

> Behold how these Christians love one another.   *Tertullian*

was focusing on the men because of the society he lived in, it is important to note that these principles are just as true for women.

4:7 **God has called us to live holy lives, not impure lives.**[NLT] The Greek word translated "called" is the exact word Paul used in Romans 8:30: "And those he predestined, he also called; those he called, he also justified; those he justified, he also glorified" (NIV; see also Romans 9:24; 1 Thessalonians 2:11-12; 2 Thessalonians 2:14). The verb means "to call forth" or "to summon." Paul always made it clear that salvation was God's initiative and that people are *called* to be his. "Calling" includes a commitment on the part of believers to *live holy lives, not impure lives.* Because it is a *call,* God is part of it, promising to help each believer have wisdom, the ability to resist temptation, and the ability to live as God desires.

HOLY, HOLY
God desires believers to be holy. A follower of Christ becomes holy or sanctified (set apart for sacred use, cleansed and made holy) through believing and obeying the Word of God (Hebrews 4:12). He or she has already accepted forgiveness through Christ's sacrificial death (Hebrews 7:26-27). But daily application of God's Word has a purifying effect on one's mind and heart. Scripture points out sin, motivates us to confess, renews our relationship with Christ, and guides us back to the right path. If you are putting off reading your Bible, you may be harboring sin in your thoughts or actions. If sexual sin is keeping you from God and his Word, confess it to God and turn away from those sinful activities.

4:8 **Therefore, anyone who refuses to live by these rules is not disobeying human teaching but is rejecting God, who gives his Holy Spirit to you.**[NLT] Clearly, to live in sexual sin is to reject God. God laid down *these rules*—basically, one rule: Sex is for married people (a man and a woman) only. *Anyone who refuses to live by* this simple rule, who treats sexual sin lightly, *is not disobeying human teaching* because human teaching changes (witness the change in sexual rules in American culture since the 1950s). To go with the flow of the surrounding culture and disregard God's rules about sexuality is tantamount to *rejecting God.*

Why does it matter so much? Paul would later write to the

believers in Corinth (another sexually immoral city and, inciden-
tally, where Paul was when he wrote the letter to the Thessalonians): "Run from sexual sin! No other sin so clearly affects the
body as this one does. For sexual immorality is a sin against your
own body" (1 Corinthians 6:18 NLT). Sexual sin is a violation of
one's own body. Paul described it as a sin that affects the body like
no other, a sin that is against one's own body, affecting not just the
flesh (promiscuous sex can lead to disease) but the whole being
and personality. Sexual sin has disastrous effects. What an entice-
ment it can be for all people—believers are not exempt.

Clearly other sins also affect the body, such as gluttony or
drunkenness, but no other sin has the same effect on the memory,
personality, or soul of a person as sexual sin. Paul argues that in
intercourse, people are united (1 Corinthians 6:16). Their spirits
are not involved in quite the same way in other sins. Also Paul
argues that a believer's body is the temple of God (1 Corinthians
6:19-20). In sexual sin, a person removes his or her body from
God's control to unite with another sinner. Thus, those people
violate God's purpose for their bodies. Satan gladly uses sexual
sin as a weapon, for he knows its power to destroy. Thus, Paul
wrote, don't walk, but "run from sexual sin!" (1 Corinthians
6:18). Believers need to exercise alertness and awareness to stay
away from places where temptation is strong, and they need to
use strong, evasive action if they find themselves entrapped.

To reject God in this area is to despise the wonderful gift of
his Holy Spirit and to reject Christ's ultimate sacrifice on sinners'
behalf. The Thessalonians had received that gift (it was given *to
you*), and they ought to have lived in thankfulness and obedience.
In Galatians 5:22-23, Paul describes the fruit of the Holy Spirit in
believers' lives. One fruit is self-control, referring to mastery over
sinful human desires and ability to show restraint. When believers surrender to the Holy Spirit, he gives them the strength to
follow God's rules. The Holy Spirit brings out the best in us, not
the worst. He reminds us of Christ's law of love and to treat our
neighbors as ourselves.

**4:9 But we don't need to write to you about the importance of
loving each other, for God himself has taught you to love one
another.**^{NLT} Paul switched gears here from exhorting the Thessalonian believers about sexual purity to exhorting those who
needed to work and not depend on others (4:11-12). He commended them that he did not need to exhort them to love one
another, for it seemed that they had learned that lesson from
God himself—most likely Paul was referring to the ministry of
the Holy Spirit. Paul used a literary device called a paralipsis.

By using it, he pretended that he was going to pass over a comment as a means of disarming his audience (see 2 Corinthians 9:1). The Christian love described by Paul is the Greek word *philadelphia.* This is the kind of love that binds people together (John 13:34-35; 1 John 2:7-8). Normally used for blood relations, the New

> Love must be learned and learned again and again; there is no end to it. Hate needs no instruction but waits only to be provoked.
> *Katherine Anne Porter*

Testament applies *philadelphia* to "faith relations" in the family of God. This is a brotherly love that should be shown among God's people. Not only did sexual purity set the believers apart from the culture around them, but so did the love they showed for one another. Indeed, it was a trademark of the first church (Acts 2:43-47; 4:32-35).

With the presence of the Holy Spirit comes his inward teaching. That "God himself has taught you to love one another" means that the Holy Spirit reminds Christians of Christ's commandment to love one another and then empowers them to do it. Christians need to be reminded daily to love each other. It is a discipline that may not come easily (see also Romans 5:5; Galatians 5:22; 1 John 4:21).

CHRISTIAN LOVE
In the Christian church, love is not only expressed by showing respect; it is also expressed through self-sacrifice and servant-hood (John 15:13). In fact, it can be defined as "selfless giving," reaching beyond friends to enemies and persecutors (Matthew 5:43-48). Love should be the unifying force and the identifying mark of the Christian community. Love is the key to walking in the light because we cannot grow spiritually while we hate others. Our growing relationship with God will result in growing relationships with others.

4:10 **Indeed, you already show your love for all the believers throughout Macedonia. Even so, dear brothers and sisters, we urge you to love them even more.**[NLT] The Thessalonian believers did not need instruction about showing God's love, but Paul urged them forward. Although their love was *already* shown not only among themselves but also toward *all the believers throughout Macedonia,* Paul begged the believers to *love them even more.* There is always more to learn about love, always more depth to be plumbed, always more ways to show love. Paul wanted them to understand that love was not an end achieved once and for all but a continual process.

4:11-12 Make it your ambition to lead a quiet life, to mind your own business and to work with your hands, just as we told you, so that your daily life may win the respect of outsiders and so that you will not be dependent on anybody.NIV Another group of believers in the church needed some warning (see also 5:14). Believers are to be responsible in all areas of life. Some of the Thessalonian Christians had adopted a life of idleness, depending on others for handouts. This did not show love for fellow believers, for these people were taking advantage of others' hard work (see Ephesians 6:6-7). The reason for their idleness is unknown, however, because a discussion of the Second Coming follows this section. These people may have decided that because Christ could return at any moment, they would just sit around and wait. They may have genuinely thought they should spend all their time working to bring others into the kingdom, but they were being a drain on their fellow believers and therefore were not loving them.

It seems that these people were not quiet about this either, so Paul first exhorted them to focus their ambition on leading *a quiet life* and minding their *own business* rather than meddling in other people's business (see also 5:14; 2 Thessalonians 3:11). The injunction to *work with your hands* may have been distasteful, for Greeks looked down on manual labor as fit only for slaves. Paul was a tent maker, however, and used his hard, manual labor as an example to all believers (2:9-11).

The reason for Paul's warning? He wanted the believers to be involved in honest labor so that they might *win the respect of outsiders* and so that they would not have to be *dependent on* others (see 1 Peter 2:12). Again, Paul had been working for these same reasons. Those who work hard to support themselves are a positive witness, both outside and inside the church (see also Ephesians 4:28).

GAINING RESPECT
Paul encouraged the believers to be contributing members, not parasites; to be self-supporting, not dependent on others. In Thessalonica some believers had abandoned their responsibilities, so their conduct could have brought condemnation on the church. Our conduct in our neighborhood and in our workplace should reflect our role as ambassadors of Christ. Does your attitude at work reflect your Christian commitment? Show enthusiasm for what you do; follow through on details assigned to you. Even in details, non-Christians will scrutinize our Christian conduct.

REMEMBER THE HOPE OF THE RESURRECTION / 4:13-18

Paul always taught people about the future—that salvation carried a promise of eternal life. He surely told his audiences that the same Jesus Christ who died, arose, and ascended would one day return. This would be Christ's "second coming" (2:19). The believers knew that this could occur at any time and that it would be unannounced.

Perhaps Paul and Silas had been forced to leave Thessalonica before they were able to finish all their teaching about the Resurrection, or perhaps this particular church had special concerns in some areas. Paul had already addressed one issue—that of earning one's keep even while awaiting Christ's return (4:11-12). The rest of chapter 4 and the first part of chapter 5 seem to be addressing several questions that had come from the church through Timothy regarding the resurrection of believers and the Second Coming.

4:13 **But we do not want you to be uninformed, brothers and sisters, about those who have died, so that you may not grieve as others do who have no hope.**NRSV The phrase "we do not want you to be uninformed" (sometimes translated, "we [or I] do not want you to be ignorant," NIV) is a phrase that Paul used several times in his letters (see Romans 1:13; 11:25; 1 Corinthians 10:1; 12:1; 2 Corinthians 1:8). These words draw attention to a topic of great importance. The question to Paul from the Thessalonian believers regarded *those who have died.* The believers had been taught that Christ would one day return and take his people to himself—every believer should be ready for that return at any moment. Apparently, in the interim, as the believers awaited Christ's return, some of them had died. The Thessalonians were wondering why this had happened before Christ's return and what would happen to those who had died when he came back. Some may have feared that believers who had died would miss the kingdom. No doubt the thought that their loved ones would not be with Christ after all caused them great sorrow. In Greek thought, the soul lived on but with no hope. It existed in sort of an ambiguous afterlife (see Ephesians 2:12).

This contrasts strongly with Paul's view (1 Corinthians 15:53-55; Philippians 1:21-23). Paul wanted the Thessalonians to understand that death is *not* the end. When Christ returns, all believers—dead and alive—will be reunited, never to suffer or die again. Believers need not *grieve as others do who have no hope.* Paul recognized that the death of loved ones naturally results in grieving, but when Christians grieve for Christians who have died, there is a difference. Their grief is not hopeless. While the pain is real, the fact is that these loved ones will be seen again as the following verses describe.

THE GREAT HOPE
Paul reminded the Thessalonian Christians that their hope was in the Resurrection. Because Jesus Christ came back to life, so will all believers. All Christians, including those who have already died when Christ returns, will live with Christ forever. Therefore, we need not despair when loved ones die or world events take a tragic turn. God will turn tragedy to triumph, poverty to riches, pain to glory, and defeat to victory. All believers throughout history will stand reunited in God's very presence, safe and secure. As Paul comforted the Thessalonians with the promise of the Resurrection, so we should comfort and reassure each other with this great hope.

4:14 **We believe that Jesus died and rose again and so we believe that God will bring with Jesus those who have fallen asleep in him.**^{NIV} Believers can have hope in the Resurrection because of what happened to Jesus. Because *Jesus died and rose again,* believers can also trust that those who have died are not lost but will be resurrected as well (see also 1 Corinthians 15:12-20). Then *God will bring with Jesus those who have fallen asleep in him* (that is, those who have died as believers). Believers who have died are in heaven already! They are presently with God and will come back with Jesus. They haven't missed out—in fact, they are enjoying God's presence. Second Corinthians 5:8 and Philippians 1:21-22 teach that believers go to heaven at death. The separation of loved ones due to death is only temporary, for those in Christ will be reunited forever.

It is interesting to note that Christians are said to "fall asleep," while Jesus "died." Jesus took upon himself the full horror of death so that he could transform it into no more than "sleep" for his followers. It is still physical death, but it is like sleep because believers do not stay dead; they are resurrected with Jesus—their souls rise immediately at death, and eventually their bodies will be raised as well (at the Second Coming, 4:16-17).

4:15 **For this we declare to you by the word of the Lord, that we who are alive, who are left until the coming of the Lord, will by no means precede those who have died.**^{NRSV} What did Paul mean when he wrote, "this we declare to you by the word of the Lord"? Either this was something that the Lord had revealed directly to Paul, or it was a teaching of Jesus that had been passed along orally by the apostles and other Christians (see John 21:25).

Nevertheless, there was no disputing what Paul was about to say. He wanted these believers to understand that neither the dead nor the living would be at any disadvantage with regard to Christ's return. All believers will share the blessings of the Resurrection. Those who have died are already with Christ and will be with him when he returns (4:14); those *who are alive,* those who are still on earth when Christ returns, *will by no means precede those who have died.* Instead, "the dead in Christ will rise first" (4:16 NIV). Knowing exactly when the dead will be raised in relation to the other events at the Second Coming is not as important as knowing why Paul wrote these words—to challenge and motivate believers to comfort and encourage one another when loved ones die. This passage can be a great comfort when any believer dies. The same love that unites believers in this life (4:9) will unite them when Christ returns and reigns for eternity.

THE KEY
The resurrection of Jesus is the key to the Christian faith. Why?

1. Just as he promised, Jesus rose from the dead. We can be confident, therefore, that he will accomplish all he has promised.
2. Jesus' bodily resurrection shows us that the living Christ is ruler of God's eternal kingdom and is not a false prophet or impostor.
3. We can be certain of our resurrection because he was resurrected. Death is not the end—there is future life.
4. The power that brought Jesus back to life is available to us to bring our spiritually dead self back to life.
5. The Resurrection is the basis for the church's witness to the world. Jesus is more than just a human leader; he is the Son of God.

4:16 **For the Lord Himself will descend from heaven with a shout, with the voice of an archangel, and with the trumpet of God. And the dead in Christ will rise first.**[NKJV] The Second Coming will occur in God's timing. He alone brings it about. Christ *the Lord Himself will descend from heaven,* for that is where he has been since his resurrection and ascension. The book of Acts describes Jesus' ascension:

> *After saying this, he was taken up into a cloud while they were watching, and they could no longer see him. As they strained to see him rising into heaven, two white-robed men suddenly stood among them. "Men of Galilee," they said, "why are you standing here staring into heaven? Jesus has been taken from you into heaven, but someday he will return from heaven in the same way you saw him go!"* (Acts 1:9-11 NLT)

In his letters Paul wrote about the Christians' waiting for Christ's return:

- "Our citizenship is in heaven. And we eagerly await a Savior from there, the Lord Jesus Christ" (Philippians 3:20 NIV).
- "They speak of how you are looking forward to the coming of God's Son from heaven—Jesus, whom God raised from the dead" (1 Thessalonians 1:10 NLT).
- "God will provide rest for you who are being persecuted and also for us when the Lord Jesus appears from heaven. He will come with his mighty angels" (2 Thessalonians 1:7 NLT).

Christ's return will be unmistakable. No one will miss it, for he will descend *with a shout, with the voice of an archangel, and with the trumpet of God.* Whether these are three different ways of referring to one sound, whether they happen simultaneously, or whether they happen in sequence is unknown. But these sounds will herald his return. Paul used distinctive imagery associated with the end times. The "shout" stands for "word of command" such as a military officer gives to his soldiers or a charioteer to his horses (see John 5:28-29 where Christ's voice calls the dead back to life). The "voice of an archangel" is the voice of a powerful angel who stands before God. An "archangel" is a high or holy angel appointed to a special task. Michael is mentioned in the New Testament (see Jude 1:9) along with Gabriel (Luke 1:19). Jewish tradition named seven archangels. Clearly the angelic hosts will be taking part in this celebration of Christ's return to take his people home (Mark 8:38). A *trumpet* blast will usher in the new heaven and earth (Revelation 11:15). The Jews would understand the significance of this because trumpets were always blown to signal the start of great festivals and other extraordinary events (see Numbers 10:10). A trumpet was also used for warning and as a military signal (see also Matthew 24:31; 1 Corinthians 15:52; Revelation 11:15). No one will miss the Second Coming—not the dead, not the living.

Then *the dead in Christ will rise first.* They will have a prominent place, for Jesus brings them with him (4:14) as part of his second coming. Although they have been with Christ since death, their bodies will be resurrected and made new. Paul later wrote to the Corinthians, "Let me reveal to you a wonderful secret. We will not all die, but we will all be transformed! It will happen in a moment, in the blink of an eye, when the last trumpet is blown. For when the trumpet sounds, those who have died will be raised to live forever" (1 Corinthians 15:51-52 NLT). At that time, when the shout sounds, the angel speaks, and the trumpet blasts,

Christ will return and the dead will rise out of the graves with their new bodies.

4:17 **Then we who are alive and remain shall be caught up together with them in the clouds to meet the Lord in the air. And thus we shall always be with the Lord.**[NKJV] After the dead have risen from their graves, the believers *who are alive and remain* on the earth *shall be caught up together with* Christ and the resurrected believers *in the clouds to meet the Lord in the air.* A reference to clouds in the Bible often symbolizes the presence of God (see Exodus 13:21; 14:19; 19:16; 24:15; 40:34-38; Mark 9:7; Acts 1:9). Christ will arrive in the clouds, and believers will be caught up to meet him in the clouds as he descends from heaven. There are differing views about whether this taking of the believers and the second coming of Christ occur at the same time, as noted below.

Clearly, all believers—whether they are alive or have died at the time of Christ's return—will be together with one another and *with the Lord* forever *(always).* The verb translated "caught up" is also used in Acts 8:39 when "the Spirit of the Lord caught Philip away" after he had baptized the Ethiopian eunuch, as well as in 2 Corinthians 12:2 when Paul wrote of being "caught up into the third heaven." This supernatural event will cause a great reunion among believers who are alive at the Second Coming and those who have already died. Both groups will experience Christ's return together. This joyous reunion will go on forever.

These words give a definite picture of the taking of the believers from the earth—they will be "caught up" (called "the Rapture")—and of the fact that that they will be with the Lord forever in heaven. There are three main views regarding the timing of the Rapture of the believers:

1. *Pretribulationists* point to the period of Tribulation (described in Revelation) that occurs before the second coming of Christ and believe that the Rapture of the believers will occur before this time of Tribulation. They believe, therefore, that believers will be in heaven while the earth goes through a time of great Tribulation. This view sees the believers meeting Christ in the clouds but places his second coming at a later time.

2. *Midtribulationists* say that the Rapture will occur at the mid-point of the time period of Tribulation. The believers will be on earth for the first half of that time of Tribulation but then will be raptured and will escape the last half, which will be a time of intense suffering. This view also sees Christ's second coming as a separate and later event.

3. *Posttribulationists* believe that the believers will remain on the earth during the time of Tribulation prior to Christ's second

THE EVENTS OF CHRIST'S RETURN

While Christians have often disagreed about what events will lead up to the return of Christ, there has been less disagreement about what will happen once he does return.

1. Christ will return visibly, with a loud command.
2. There will be an unmistakable cry from an angel.
3. There will be a trumpet fanfare such as has never been heard.
4. Believers in Christ who are dead will rise from their graves.
5. Believers who are alive will be caught up in the clouds to meet Christ.

coming. Then when Christ returns in the clouds, believers will be caught up to be with him. This is also the Second Coming, when Christ comes to judge and set up his kingdom.

This verse, 4:17, is a key verse for those who make the Rapture a distinct event from the return of Christ to reign (see also John 14:1-3; 1 Corinthians 15:51-53; 2 Thessalonians 2:1).

While Christians may differ regarding the timing of this Rapture, all believe that it will happen and that it will be a joyous reunion of all believers, living and dead. Paul's point was not to give his readers a timeline or a literal description of how all the end-times events would fit together. Instead, he wanted to reassure the Thessalonians that their fellow believers who had died would not miss out on Christ's return and eternal kingdom.

4:18 **Therefore encourage one another with these words.**^NRSV The Thessalonians did not need to continue worrying about the spiritual state of those who had died. Paul explained to these believers that being dead or alive at the return of Christ would make no difference, for Christ would bring all his people together to be with him forever. Instead of worrying, they should *encourage one another with these words* (see also 3:7; 5:11). No one is beyond God's power—no believer will be left out or forgotten. Even in the face of death, believers know that their Lord is ultimately triumphant.

SPREAD THE WORD
Paul said to encourage one another. Do you need encouragement? Paul's words offer joy and hope in times of trouble, and he bases his confidence on what God has done for us in Christ Jesus. Our hope is not only for the future: Eternal life begins when we trust Christ and join God's family. No matter what pain or trial we face in this life, we know it is not our final experience. Eventually we will live with Christ forever. As we share these words of encouragement with others, we ourselves are built up in our faith.

1 Thessalonians 5

Certain questions have perplexed Christians across the ages. All are concerned when loved ones die, and they wonder when they will see them again. All are also concerned about the Day of Judgment and what that will mean for them. The end of chapter 4 addresses the bereavement issue, stating that believers who have died will not be left out of the Second Coming. The first part of chapter 5 addresses the issue of the Day of Judgment and how believers can prepare for it.

This section (5:1-11) and the previous section (4:13-18) have been the subject of ongoing debate. Some have interpreted them as describing two separate events: (1) 4:13-18 refers to the Second Coming, with emphasis on the Rapture of the saints (4:17); and (2) 5:1-11 refers to the period of Tribulation (the Day of the Lord, 5:2). Others view these two sections as topically distinct but not necessarily indicating two events. They say that Paul emphasized the Resurrection in 4:13-18 and the Judgment in 5:1-11. The purpose of the first section is to reassure believers who have lost loved ones; the purpose of the second section is to warn believers to be spiritually alert and morally prepared.

5:1-2 **Now concerning how and when all this will happen, dear brothers and sisters, we don't really need to write you. For you know quite well that the day of the Lord's return will come unexpectedly, like a thief in the night.**[NLT] The phrase "day of the Lord's return" refers to a future time when God will intervene directly and dramatically in world affairs. Predicted and discussed often in the Old Testament (see Isaiah 13:6-13; Joel 2:28-32; Amos 5:18-20; Zephaniah 1:14-18), the "day of the Lord" will include both punishment and blessing. Christ will judge sin and set up his eternal kingdom. Paul had already taught at length about this day and had just answered the Thessalonian believers' question concerning fellow believers who had died (4:13-18). They knew that the timing of this event was unknown, for Paul had already explained to them that it *will come unexpectedly, like a*

THE SECOND COMING

(Verses quoted from the NLT)

Reference	*Selected Quote*
Matthew 24:27	"For as the lightning flashes in the east and shines to the west, so it will be when the Son of Man comes."
Matthew 26:64 (see also Mark 14:62)	"In the future you will see the Son of Man in the place of power at God's right hand and coming on the clouds of heaven."
Mark 13:24-27	"The sun will be darkened, the moon will give no light, the stars will fall from the sky. . . . And he will send out his angels to gather his chosen ones from all over the world."
Luke 21:25-28	"And here on earth the nations will be in turmoil, perplexed by the roaring seas and strange tides. People will be terrified at what they see coming upon the earth."
1 Corinthians 15:51-53	"We will not all die, but we will all be transformed! . . . For when the trumpet sounds, those who have died will be raised to live forever. And we who are living will also be transformed."
Philippians 3:20-21	"We are citizens of heaven. . . . And we are eagerly waiting for him to return as our Savior. He will take our weak mortal bodies and change them into glorious bodies like his own."
Colossians 3:4	"And when Christ, who is your life, is revealed to the whole world, you will share in all his glory."
1 Thessalonians 2:19	"After all, what gives us hope and joy, and what will be our proud reward and crown as we stand before our Lord Jesus when he returns? It is you!"
1 Thessalonians 4:13-18	"When Jesus returns, God will bring back with him the believers who have died. . . . For the Lord himself will come down from heaven. . . . First, the Christians who have died will rise from their graves. Then, together with them, we who are still alive and remain on the earth will be caught up in the clouds to meet the Lord in the air."
2 Thessalonians 1:6-10	"He will come with his mighty angels, in flaming fire, bringing judgment on those who don't know God and on those who refuse to obey the Good News of our Lord Jesus."

2 Thessalonians 2:1-17	"That day will not come until there is a great rebellion against God and the man of lawlessness is revealed. . . . He will exalt himself and defy everything that people call god. . . . Jesus will kill him with the breath of his mouth and destroy him by the splendor of his coming."
1 Timothy 6:14-15	"For at just the right time Christ will be revealed from heaven by the blessed and only almighty God, the King of all kings and Lord of all lords."
Titus 2:12-13	"We should live in this evil world with wisdom, righteousness, and devotion to God, while we look forward with hope to that wonderful day when the glory of our great God and Savior, Jesus Christ, will be revealed."
Hebrews 9:28	"Christ died once for all time as a sacrifice to take away the sins of many people. He will come again, not to deal with our sins, but to bring salvation to all who are eagerly waiting for him."
James 5:7-8	"Be patient as you wait for the Lord's return. . . . Take courage, for the coming of the Lord is near."
1 Peter 1:7, 13	"So when your faith remains strong through many trials, it will bring you much praise and glory and honor on the day when Jesus Christ is revealed to the whole world. . . . Look forward to the gracious salvation that will come to you when Jesus Christ is revealed to the world."
2 Peter 3:1-14	"A day is like a thousand years to the Lord, and a thousands years is like a day. The Lord isn't really being slow about his promise, as some people think. No, he is being patient for your sake. He does not want anyone to be destroyed, but wants everyone to repent. But the day of the Lord will come as unexpectedly as a thief. Then the heavens will pass away with a terrible noise, and the very elements themselves will disappear in fire."
1 John 2:28–3:2	"Remain in fellowship with Christ so that when he returns, you will be full of courage and not shrink back from him in shame. . . . We are already God's children, but he has not yet shown us what we will be like when Christ appears. But we do know that we will be like him, for we will see him as he really is."
Jude 1:14	"Listen! The Lord is coming with countless thousands of his holy ones."
Revelation 1:7	"Look! He comes with the clouds of heaven. And everyone will see him."

thief in the night (see also 2 Peter 3:10; Revelation 3:3; 16:15).
Paul was the first to associate the "day of the Lord" with the
coming of Jesus Christ (see 1 Corinthians 1:8; 5:5; 2 Corinthians
1:14).

Jesus had discussed his second coming and at one point had
compared it to the coming of a thief:

> *No one knows about that day or hour, not even the angels in*
> *heaven, nor the Son, but only the Father. . . . But understand*
> *this: If the owner of the house had known at what time of night*
> *the thief was coming, he would have kept watch and would not*
> *have let his house be broken into. So you also must be ready,*
> *because the Son of Man will come at an hour when you do not*
> *expect him.* (Matthew 24:36, 43-44 NIV)

Some have attempted to pinpoint dates or prove how certain
present events fulfill prophecy. Jesus made it clear and Paul
reiterated, however, that no one knows when Christ will return.
It will be unexpected and on God's timetable. Jesus predicted
that before his return many believers would be misled by false
teachers claiming to have revelations from God (Mark 13:5-6).
According to Scripture, the one clear sign of Christ's return
will be his unmistakable appearance in the clouds. This will be
seen by all people (Mark 13:26; Revelation 1:7). In other words,
believers do not have to wonder whether a certain person is the
Messiah or whether the times in which they live are the end
times. When Jesus returns, everyone will know beyond a doubt
because it will be evident. Beware of groups that claim special
knowledge of the last days because no one knows when that time
will be.

WELCOME MAT
Paul said Christ will come unexpectedly. Efforts to determine the
date of the Second Coming are foolish. Don't be misled by anyone who claims to know. The Bible says that no one knows and
that even believers will be surprised. The Lord will return suddenly and unexpectedly, so believers should be ready! Christ's
second coming will be swift and sudden. There will be no opportunity for last-minute repentance or bargaining. The choice you
have already made will determine your eternal destiny. Suppose
he were to return today. How would he find you living? Are you
ready to meet him? Live each day prepared to welcome Christ.

**5:3 While people are saying, "Peace and safety," destruction will
come on them suddenly, as labor pains on a pregnant woman,
and they will not escape.**^{NIV} The comparison of Christ's coming

to a thief (5:1-2) reveals that it will be sudden and unexpected; the comparison of it to *labor pains on a pregnant woman* indicates that it will be unavoidable (see also Mark 13:8). Some who will not be waiting for Christ will think that everything is safe—they will be lulled into a false sense of *peace and safety* (see also Jeremiah 6:14; 8:11; Ezekiel 13:10). However, they will find themselves facing sudden *destruction.* This word "destruction" *(olethpos)* is also used in 2 Thessalonians 1:9 and refers to separation from God: "They will be punished with everlasting destruction and shut out from the presence of the Lord and from the majesty of his power" (NIV). When Christ returns, that *will* be the end—there will be no reprieves, no second chances, no *escape.*

In order to be ready for the Second Coming, the Thessalonian believers may have thought it would only make sense to know when that coming would be. So Paul further explained that the Second Coming is certain and will be sudden and unavoidable. So how are believers to be ready? The following verses explain.

WE HAVE WORK TO DO
It is good that we don't know exactly when Christ will return. If we knew the precise date, we might be tempted to be lazy in our work for Christ. Worse yet, we might plan to keep sinning and then turn to God right at the end. Heaven is not our only goal; we have work to do here. Christians must keep on doing God's work until death or until we see the unmistakable return of our Savior.

5:4-5 But you, beloved, are not in darkness, for that day to surprise you like a thief; for you are all children of light and children of the day; we are not of the night or of darkness.NRSV The *beloved* believers in Thessalonica were *not in darkness;* that is, they were not ignorant of what was to occur. God has chosen not to tell his people everything about Christ's return, but believers know all that they need to know. God has not left his people "in darkness" so that they will be totally surprised when Christ comes back. From the moment Christ ascended into heaven, the promise remained that someday, just as he went, he would return (Acts 1:11). For believers, that promise is not scary; instead, it is a promise of hope. Because believers *are all children of light and children of the day,* that return will be a time of great joy.

The contrasts of "light" and "darkness" and "day" and "night" are often used in the Bible to describe the difference between good and evil, between God's people and the people of the world.

First John 1:5 says that "God is light, and there is no darkness in him at all" (NLT). Light represents what is good, pure, true, holy, and reliable. Darkness represents what is sinful and evil. God is perfectly holy and true, and he alone can guide people out of the darkness of sin. Light is also related to truth in that light exposes whatever exists, whether it is good or bad. In the dark, good and evil look alike; in the light, they can be clearly distinguished. Just as darkness cannot exist in the presence of light, sin cannot exist in the presence of a holy God.

"Children of light," God's children, have nothing to fear regarding the Second Coming—although they are responsible to be ready.

GET READY
Paul warned Christians not to be surprised by Christ's return. The only way for believers not to be surprised is to be morally ready and spiritually vigilant at all times (see 5:6-8). Knowing that Christ's return will be sudden and unexpected should motivate us to always be prepared. We are not to live irresponsibly—sitting and waiting, doing nothing, seeking self-serving pleasure, or using the time until he returns as an excuse not to do God's work of building his kingdom. No one should develop a false sense of security based on precise calculations of events or let their curiosity about the end times divert them from doing God's work. Are you working, serving, and waiting?

5:6-7 **So be on your guard, not asleep like the others. Stay alert and be clearheaded. Night is the time when people sleep and drinkers get drunk.**^NLT Usually thieves break into homes at night when everyone is sleeping. Jesus' second coming *will* happen, and it will happen with surprise like a thief breaking in, but God's people should *be on . . . guard, not asleep.* The way to be ready for Jesus' return is not in knowing when he will return, for he won't give that information. Instead, readiness lies in being *alert* and *clearheaded.* The children of the light will be awake and ready when the Lord returns. Paul describes those who constantly expect the Lord to return at any moment. They are not dallying in sin or falling into temptation or being waylaid by their own doubts. We also must walk close to God in daily fellowship with him so that at the Second Coming we will be ready.

This contrasts with the rest of the world, the *others* of the "darkness" and of the "night" who are *asleep* at the Lord's return. The word translated "asleep" *(katheudo)* is used for moral indifference (see Mark 13:36; Ephesians 5:14). These people aren't waiting for the Lord, aren't caring that he could return, and are even getting *drunk* (the opposite of *clearheaded*), a metaphor for their moral indifference toward the holy God. "Clearheaded" also means "self-controlled" (NIV) and further implies being ready rather than muddled in one's thinking. Because unbelievers are people of the "darkness" and of the "night," their lives are focused on their own pleasures and obsessions and not on alertness and moral readiness for the coming of Christ.

> Christ designed that the day of his coming should be hid from us, that being in suspense, we might be, as it were, upon the watch.
>
> *Martin Luther*

5:8 But since we belong to the day, let us be self-controlled, putting on faith and love as a breastplate, and the hope of salvation as a helmet.[NIV] People who *belong to the day,* the believers who are living in the "light" of God, have a whole different reason to be alive. Life is not all about personal pleasure but about loving and serving God and getting to know him better. The reward for being God's children is that when he returns, he will take his people to eternal blessing. This means that in this sinful world, the world of "darkness" and "night," believers have to be different. First of all, they must *be self-controlled,* for self-control can keep people from many sins—especially the sexual sins described in 4:3-8. Self-control helps a person be ready for Christ's return as it helps him or her stay away from sin.

In addition, however, believers need to realize that they are in a battle. Spiritual warfare is very real, and Satan does not easily accept people's leaving his kingdom for God's kingdom. So believers must be armed and ready, like soldiers, *putting on faith and love as a breastplate, and the hope of salvation as a helmet.* To the Ephesians, Paul had written about the armor believers need for their spiritual battle:

> *Put on the full armor of God so that you can take your stand against the devil's schemes. For our struggle is not against flesh and blood, but against the rulers, against the authorities, against the powers of this dark world and against the spiritual forces of evil in the heavenly realms. Therefore put on the full armor of God, so that when the day of evil comes, you may be able to stand your ground, and after you have done everything, to stand.* (Ephesians 6:11-13 NIV)

Believers face a powerful army whose goal is to defeat Christ's church. Those who believe in Christ are assured of victory. They must engage in the struggle until Christ returns, however, because Satan is constantly battling against all who are on the Lord's side.

Christians need supernatural power to defeat Satan, and God has
provided this by giving his Holy Spirit and his armor for protection. In Ephesians, "righteousness" is the breastplate, while here
Paul used "faith and love" as the breastplate. Probably the anal-
ogy cannot be pressed too far other than to say that believers have
supernatural armor for the battle, but they must put it on. Believers have faith and love to protect their hearts and hope to keep
their minds focused on the goal—God's eternal kingdom.

5:9-10 **For God did not appoint us to suffer wrath but to receive salvation through our Lord Jesus Christ. He died for us so that,
whether we are awake or asleep, we may live together with
him.**NIV In order to wear "hope" as a helmet (5:8), believers must
know in what (or in whom) they are hoping. Christians' hope lies
secure because *God* is in charge. He has made the decision and
did not appoint [his people] to suffer wrath. Because God has
ordained it this way, it is certain. God's wrath is very real. Sin
will be punished, and those who have refused his offer of forgiveness will indeed suffer God's wrath (Revelation 20:11-15).

Those who argue for the Rapture (4:17) to occur before the
Tribulation starts on earth interpret these verses to refer to the
beginning of the outpouring of God's wrath in the seven-year
period of Tribulation. But "wrath" as used here (the Greek word
is *orge*) refers to the Day of the Lord, the final judgment.

God's people will not face the condemnation that their sins
deserve, however. Instead, they will *receive salvation* because
they have put their faith in Jesus' sacrifice on the cross for forgiveness of their sins. This salvation was offered *through our
Lord Jesus Christ.* He said, "I am the way, the truth, and the
life. No one can come to the Father except through me" (John
14:6 NLT). How did Jesus accomplish this? Through his death.
Jesus, the sinless Son of God, *died for us,* died in the place of
sinful humanity, to spare us from punishment. Those who accept
Jesus' sacrifice *receive salvation.*

Why did Jesus have to die? Jesus' death on the cross sealed
a new covenant between God and people. The old covenant
involved forgiveness of sins through the blood of an animal sacrifice (see Exodus 24:6-8). Instead of a spotless lamb on the altar,
Jesus offered himself, the spotless Lamb of God, as a sacrifice
that would forgive sin once and for all. Jesus was the final sacrifice for sins, and his blood sealed the new agreement between
God and people. Now all are welcomed to come to God *through
our Lord Jesus Christ.* Through his death, the promise was sealed.

Christ's sacrifice for sins was not an afterthought, not something God decided to do after the world had spun out of control.

All-knowing, eternal God set this plan in motion long before the world was created. First Peter 1:18-21 says:

You know that it was not with perishable things such as silver or gold that you were redeemed from the empty way of life handed down to you from your forefathers, but with the precious blood of Christ, a lamb without blemish or defect. He was chosen before the creation of the world, but was revealed in these last times for your sake. Through him you believe in God, who raised him from the dead and glorified him, and so your faith and hope are in God. (NIV)

The hope rests secure *whether* believers *are awake or asleep* at Christ's return. Salvation is a certainty because the Christ who is coming is the same Christ who died for sinners. All believers—those who have died and those who are still alive—will *live together with* God in heaven. God has appointed this to come to pass, and no power can change his plan (read Revelation 21–22).

ENCOURAGING WORDS
As you near the end of a long race, your legs ache, your throat burns, and your whole body cries out for you to stop. This is when friends and fans are most valuable. Their encouragement helps you push through the pain to the finish line. In the same way, Christians are to encourage one another. A word of encouragement offered at the right moment can mean the difference between finishing well and collapsing along the way. Look around you. Be sensitive to others' need for encouragement, and offer supportive words or actions.

5:11 Therefore encourage one another and build up each other, as indeed you are doing.NRSV The words "encourage one another" repeat Paul's words in 4:18. Despite persecution and their sorrow over fellow believers who had died, the Christians needed to *encourage one another* about the certainty of their future reunion with all believers who had gone on before (4:13-18) and the promise of eternal life through Jesus Christ (5:9-10). They ought also to *build up each other* in the faith as they dealt with the difficult issues and to seek to be ready for Christ's return (5:1-8). Apparently the Thessalonians were already doing this, so Paul took note of that fact; yet he wanted them to continue to do so. Believers will never stop needing encouragement or building up. Just as one believer receives encouragement, he or she at another time will be in a position to offer it. The mutual giving and receiving in the body of Christ keep the church strong against the forces that attack it. God's people always need to stand together with one another as they anticipate their Savior's return.

PAUL'S FINAL INSTRUCTIONS / 5:12-28

Because God is a loving Father, all who join his family become "brothers and sisters." Paul used this familial term (the Greek word *adelphotes* is translated various ways) five times in the last section of this letter (5:12, 14, 25, 26, and 27). Clearly, Paul wanted to leave these final instructions to all the believers so that they could continue to build one another up (5:11). This section focuses on three parts of life in a local church and how the relationships ought to work—from the pastors and leadership to the fellowship and responsibilities of the believers and finally to how they ought to worship. The instructions are as vital to churches today as they were in the first century.

5:12 **Dear brothers and sisters, honor those who are your leaders in the Lord's work. They work hard among you and give you spiritual guidance.**^{NLT} The *brothers and sisters* in the church needed to show *honor* to those in leadership in order for everything to function smoothly. The word "honor" is also translated "respect." These *leaders in the Lord's work* probably were the elders, who held positions of leadership and responsibility. Elders were church officers providing supervision, protection, discipline, instruction, and direction for the other believers. "Elder" simply means "older." Both Greeks and Jews gave positions of great honor to wise older men, and the Christian church continued this pattern of leadership. Elders carried great responsibility, and they were expected to be good examples. These men worked hard among the believers and deserved to be honored. Paul expressed a similar thought in his letter to Timothy: "The elders who direct the affairs of the church well are worthy of double honor, especially those whose work is preaching and teaching" (1 Timothy 5:17 NIV).

The leadership structure in local churches began very early, for as Paul planted a church and then moved on, he needed to leave behind an organized group of believers (see Acts 11:30; 14:23; 1 Timothy 4:14; Titus 1:5; James 5:14; 1 Peter 5:1). Paul could not stay in each church, but he knew that these new churches needed strong spiritual leadership. Leaders were chosen to teach sound doctrine, help believers mature spiritually, and equip believers to live for Jesus Christ despite opposition. Acts 14:23 describes Paul and Barnabas's return to some of the churches that they had planted. Part of the reason that Paul and Barnabas risked their lives to return to these cities was to organize the churches' leadership, helping believers get organized with spiritual leaders who could help them grow. The churches needed Spirit-led leaders, both laypersons and pastors.

Timothy may have also reported back to Paul some concern regarding a lack of respect by the Christians for their leaders. Perhaps the leaders had been giving *spiritual guidance* and in so doing been the target of criticism. It may have been that the leaders' warnings were not being heeded or that at times the leaders had been a bit overbearing in their dealings with sin in the congregation. The injunction to "live in peace" in 5:13 (NIV) includes all believers, even their leaders. If the leaders had not exercised their authority delicately enough, they may have been met with resistance. They needed to learn how to lead gently and with the heart of a servant. Even so, Paul explained that these men had been put in positions of responsibility for a reason; thus, believers should respect and heed their words.

STRONG SUPPORT
Paul instructed the church to honor its leaders. Faithful church leaders should be supported and appreciated. Too often they are targets for criticism because the congregation has unrealistic expectations. How do you treat your church leaders? Do you enjoy finding fault, or do you show your appreciation? Do they receive enough financial support to allow them to live without worry and to provide for the needs of their families? Jesus and Paul emphasized the importance of supporting those who lead and teach us.

How can you show respect to and hold in the "highest regard" your pastor and other church leaders? Express your appreciation, tell them how you have been helped by their leadership and teaching, and thank them for their ministry in your life. If you say nothing, how will they know where you stand? Remember, they need and deserve your support and love.

5:13 Hold them in the highest regard in love because of their work. Live in peace with each other.NIV In addition to honoring their leaders (5:12), believers are also to *hold them in the highest regard in love.* "The highest regard" conveys a superlative forcefulness that left Paul's readers with no doubt about his meaning. Leaders are not to be ignored or argued with; they are to be held in highest esteem—not with fear but with love. These leaders are to be respected and loved, not just because of their position of responsibility, but also *because of their work.* When believers respect their leaders and join them in their work for God's kingdom, the church will grow. Of course, it also helps if leaders do not have to spend all their time dealing with internal conflicts; hence, Paul reminded believers to *live in peace with each other.* The command to "live in peace" includes the leaders as well. All are to work together to build the kingdom and to serve one another. The best way for this "peace" to occur is for all believers to serve with their God-given gifts, to let others use *their* gifts, and then to respect and love one another for what God is doing through them.

5:14 **Brothers and sisters, we urge you to warn those who are lazy. Encourage those who are timid. Take tender care of those who are weak. Be patient with everyone.**^{NLT} While the leaders have special responsibility to guide the church, believers *(brothers and sisters)* are not exempt from their responsibility to care for one another. Paul singled out three groups in this church and "urged" believers to look after or deal with them—but in different ways.

First, they were to *warn those who [were] lazy.* The word "warn" is also in 5:12 and means to firmly admonish, particularly in the areas of sin. They were to warn lazy, idle believers. The word translated "lazy" is used only in the letters to the Thessalonians (see also 2 Thessalonians 3:6-7, 11) and seems to have been a particular concern for this church. The Greek word translated "lazy" *(ataktous)* was used for soldiers who would not stay in the ranks. These people had set themselves outside the prescribed pattern for the church—everyone else was working and serving, but they would not. Second Thessalonians 3:11 calls these people "busybodies" (NIV). The problem with idle people is that because they are not busy enough with valuable activities, they usually stir up trouble of one kind or another. These people need to be warned to get back in among the believers and use their God-given gifts in service for the kingdom.

Second, they were to *encourage those who [were] timid.* The word "encourage" is also used in 2:12, where Paul described his ministry among the Thessalonians. The Greek word translated "encourage" *(paraklesis)* means to come alongside with helpful instruction and insight. The lazy need to be warned, but the "timid" need to be encouraged. The "timid" are the fearful people who lack confidence—perhaps in themselves or even in their faith. They have become discouraged or worried, possibly by persecution or by the deaths of their fellow believers (4:13). These people need loving instruction from their fellow believers to calm their fears and to build their confidence.

Third, they were to *take tender care of those who [were] weak.* The word translated "take tender care" is *antechesthe* (also

translated simply as "help") and means to hold on to these
people, wrap arms around them, and cling to them. This is the
kind of help suggested for the spiritually "weak," those weak in
faith, those in need (such as financial need), or those who might
be struggling with the sins associated with paganism that Paul
wrote about in 4:3-8. These might be struggling, needy, or immature Christians who need the arms of strong fellow believers to
guide them, give them support, and let them know they are not
alone. See also Romans 5:6; 14:1; 1 Corinthians 8:9.

Paul's advice is simply to use the right medicine. For example:

- It would not work to "take tender care" of a "lazy" person; that
  person would not appreciate it and would remain unchanged.
- It would not work to "warn" a "timid" person; that person is
  of fragile self-esteem anyway, and a warning would only scare
  him or her away.
- It would not work to "encourage" a truly "weak" person to
  press on to greater things; that would show callousness to the
  person's real need. The one trying to encourage may be doing
  so because it takes far less effort and involvement than taking
  "tender care" of that person as Paul prescribed.

Finally, being *patient with everyone* is the glue that holds relationships together. In any group where a variety of people come
together, godly patience will be required of everyone. Believers
cannot write off the lazy, timid, or weak even if they do require
a lot of time and energy. On the contrary, great patience must be
exercised. The word for "patient" *(makrothymia)* is also translated
"long-suffering." This is an attribute of God (see Exodus 34:6;
Psalm 103:8), a fruit of the Holy Spirit in believers (Galatians
5:22), and a characteristic of love (1 Corinthians 13:4). God is
patient with people, and so Christians should be. In addition, God
has given his Spirit to help his people be patient with one another.

THE RIGHT MEDICINE
Don't loaf around with the idle; warn them. Don't yell at the timid
and weak; encourage and help them. At times it's difficult to
distinguish between idleness and timidity. Two people may be
doing nothing—one out of laziness and the other out of shy-
ness or fear of doing something wrong. The key to ministry is
sensitivity: sensing the condition of each person and offering the
appropriate remedy for each situation. You can't effectively help
until you know the problem. You can't apply the medicine until
you know what is causing the pain.

5:15 **Make sure that nobody pays back wrong for wrong, but always try to be kind to each other and to everyone else.**^{NIV} To a church under persecution, the command against retaliation is especially poignant. *Make sure that nobody pays back wrong for wrong.* Personal revenge and retaliation are clearly forbidden to those who call themselves followers of Christ. Jesus said, "But I tell you, Do not resist an evil person. If someone strikes you on the right cheek, turn to him the other also. . . . But I tell you: Love your enemies and pray for those who persecute you" (Matthew 5:39, 44 NIV). To many Jews of Jesus' day, these statements were offensive. Any Messiah who would turn the other cheek was not the military leader they wanted to lead a revolt against Rome. Because they were under Roman oppression, they wanted retaliation against their hated enemies. Instead, Jesus suggested a new, radical response to injustice. Instead of demanding rights, give them up freely! According to Jesus, it is more important to give justice and mercy than to receive it.

To the Romans, Paul had written:

> *Do not repay anyone evil for evil. Be careful to do what is right in the eyes of everybody. If it is possible, as far as it depends on you, live at peace with everyone. Do not take revenge, my friends, but leave room for God's wrath, for it is written: "It is mine to avenge; I will repay," says the Lord. On the contrary: "If your enemy is hungry, feed him; if he is thirsty, give him something to drink. In doing this, you will heap burning coals on his head." Do not be overcome by evil, but overcome evil with good.* (Romans 12:17-21 NIV)

In addition, there would be times when relationships between believers would be strained. They would also need to remember that they should never pay back "wrong for wrong" but should *always try to be kind to each other and to everyone else*— including those in the church and those outside, even their enemies. That believers should "always try" indicates a lifestyle of kindness that should permeate all their dealings with others.

5:16 **Rejoice always.**^{NKJV} The next three verses give three simple ingredients that believers ought to daily mix into their lives: joy, prayer, and thanks. When these three qualities are present, believers will be vibrant witnesses to a needy world.

Paul counseled this persecuted church to *rejoice always*. Paul had learned the secret of being joyful,

> Joy seems to be distilled from a strange mixture of challenge, risk and hope.
>
> *Keith Miller*

even in the middle of great trial and suffering (verses quoted
from NIV):

- Acts 16:25: "About midnight Paul and Silas were praying and
  singing hymns to God, and the other prisoners were listening to
  them."
- Romans 5:3: "Not only so, but we also rejoice in our sufferings,
  because we know that suffering produces perseverance."
- 2 Corinthians 6:4-10: "Rather, as servants of God we commend
  ourselves in every way: in great endurance; in troubles, hardships and distresses; in beatings, imprisonments and riots; in
  hard work, sleepless nights and hunger; in purity, understanding, patience and kindness; in the Holy Spirit and in
  sincere love; in truthful speech and in the power of God;
  with weapons of righteousness in the right hand and in the
  left; through glory and dishonor, bad report and good report;
  genuine, yet regarded as impostors; known, yet regarded as
  unknown; dying, and yet we live on; beaten, and yet not killed;
  sorrowful, yet always rejoicing; poor, yet making many rich;
  having nothing, and yet possessing everything."
- 2 Corinthians 12:10: "That is why, for Christ's sake, I delight
  in weaknesses, in insults, in hardships, in persecutions, in
  difficulties. For when I am weak, then I am strong."
- Colossians 1:24: "Now I rejoice in what was suffered for
  you, and I fill up in my flesh what is still lacking in regard
  to Christ's afflictions, for the sake of his body, which is the
  church."

Paul had just commanded the believers to love one another and
then to rejoice. Interestingly, when Jesus spoke to his disciples
about loving one another, he also talked to them about joy:

> *As the Father has* loved *me, so I have* loved *you; abide in
> my* love. *If you keep my commandments, you will abide in
> my* love*, just as I have kept my Father's commandments and
> abide in his* love. *I have said these things to you so that my* joy
> *may be in you, and that your* joy *may be complete. This is my
> commandment, that you* love *one another as I have* loved *you.
> No one has greater* love *than this, to lay down one's life for
> one's friends.* (John 15:9-13 NRSV, emphasis added)

True joy transcends the rolling waves of circumstance. Joy
comes from a consistent relationship with Jesus Christ. When
believers' lives are intertwined with Christ, he will help them to
walk through adversity without sinking into debilitating lows and
to manage prosperity without moving into deceptive highs. The
joy of living with Jesus Christ daily will keep believers rejoicing

"always." They can rejoice because of their sure salvation and their future hope. Nothing that happens on this earth can compare with the glory that awaits God's people.

> Prayer is a shield to the soul, a sacrifice to God, and a scourge to Satan.
> *John Bunyan*

But believers are not required to conjure up this joy, for the ability to rejoice has been given to them as a gift—one fruit of the Holy Spirit is joy (Galatians 5:22; see also Romans 14:17).

REAL JOY
Our joy, prayers, and thankfulness should not fluctuate with our circumstances or feelings. Obeying these three commands—be joyful, pray continually, and give thanks—often goes against our natural inclinations. When we make a conscious decision to do what God says, however, we will begin to see people in a new perspective. When we do God's will, we will find it easier to be joyful and thankful.

5:17 Pray without ceasing.^{NKJV} Paul did not expect believers to spend all their time on their knees or with their eyes closed when he said they should *pray without ceasing*. In fact, he was quite adamant that everyone had work to do (5:14; 2 Thessalonians 3:6-7, 11). It is possible, however, for believers to have a prayerful attitude at all times. This attitude is built upon acknowledging dependence on God, realizing his presence within, and determining to obey him fully. Then it will be natural to pray frequent, spontaneous, short prayers. Prayer is not to be done by the church leader only, nor is it meant to be carried out only in worship services. Instead, prayer can be a part of every believer's daily walk, and Paul noted how important this would be for one's spiritual life (Romans 12:12; Ephesians 6:19). Jesus told his disciples that "they should always pray and not give up" (Luke 18:1 NIV). Believers should pray together in worship, spend time alone with God in prayer, and also pray to God throughout each day as the desire to rejoice or the need for help arises.

5:18 In everything give thanks; for this is the will of God in Christ Jesus for you.^{NKJV} Notice that Paul did not say "for" everything give thanks, but *in* everything. Evil will happen to believers, and it does not come from God, so they should not thank him for it. But when evil strikes, they can still be thankful for God's presence and for the good he will accomplish through the distress. Paul had learned that "God causes everything to work together for the good of those who love God and are called according to his purpose for them" (Romans 8:28 NLT). Usually God uses difficult times to build people's character and strengthen their faith. It is easy to give thanks for the blessings; it is more difficult to give thanks for the blessings in disguise. By far the most difficult task is to give thanks in *everything*—even the situations that make no sense or are extremely painful. Yet this difficult task has been assigned to all believers *for this is the will of God in Christ Jesus for you.* Learning to give thanks in everything means learning to trust God completely, knowing that he is in charge, and understanding that all that happens is part of a larger picture that believers may not see. When a believer can give thanks so willingly, he or she has trusted that God is completely in control of all situations and is working out his will.

WITHOUT STOPPING
Have you ever grown tired of praying for something or someone? Paul said that believers should pray without ceasing. A Christian's persistence is an expression of faith that God answers prayer. Faith shouldn't die if the answers come slowly, for the delay may be God's way of working his will. When you feel tired of praying, know that God is present, always listening, always answering—maybe not in ways you had hoped but in ways that he knows are best.

5:19 Do not stifle the Holy Spirit.^{NLT} Other versions translate this verse, "Do not put out the Spirit's fire" (NIV) or "Do not quench the Spirit" (NRSV; see also Ephesians 4:30). "Stifle" means to douse a fire, so to *stifle the Holy Spirit* would be to forbid or restrain his work. By warning the believers *not* to stifle the Holy Spirit, Paul may have meant that the believers in Thessalonica should not grieve the Spirit through any of the sins that had been mentioned in this letter—immorality and laziness, for example. More likely, Paul may have been referring to a situation in the church in which some of the believers had been limiting or forbidding the exercise of certain spiritual gifts, such as prophecy or speaking in tongues. Paul warned that no one should ignore or toss aside the gifts the Holy Spirit gives. The following

For three things I thank God every day of my life: thanks that he has vouchsafed me knowledge of his works; deep thanks that he has set in my darkness the lamp of faith; deep, deepest thanks that I have another life to look forward to—a life joyous with light and flowers and heavenly song.   *Helen Keller* verses specifically mention prophecy and tongues: 5:20; 1 Corinthians 14:1-19, 39. Sometimes the immature use of spiritual gifts causes divisions in a church. Rather than trying to solve the problems, these believers may have been attempting to stifle those gifts. This would only impoverish them, however. No one should stifle the Holy Spirit's work in anyone's life; all Christians should encourage the full expression of these gifts to benefit the whole body of Christ. (See the commentary on 2 Timothy 1:6 in *Life Application Bible Commentary: 1 & 2 Timothy / Titus,* pages 156–157.)

5:20-21 **Do not treat prophecies with contempt. Test everything. Hold on to the good.**[NIV] God appointed certain people as prophets to the church (1 Corinthians 12:10, 28). These people had special gifts in ministering God's messages to his people. At times they would foretell the future (Acts 11:28; 21:9-11), but more often they would exhort, encourage, and strengthen God's people (Acts 15:32). God spoke through prophets—inspiring them with specific messages for particular times and places.

The gift of prophecy had not so much to do with predicting future events as it had to do with bringing a message from God under the direction of the Holy Spirit to the body of believers. This gift provided insight, warning, correction, and encouragement (see 1 Corinthians 14:3). The Thessalonians apparently were treating some prophecies—perhaps the warnings and corrections with which they did not agree—*with contempt.* These prophecies would have been heard in the context of worship, although opinions differ on what these entailed. The Reformers (Calvin, Luther) believed that sermons are the exercise of the gift of prophecy. Other scholars say that prophecy refers to spontaneous, Spirit-inspired messages that are orally delivered in the congregation for the edification and encouragement of the body of Christ.

The gift of prophecy is highly regarded. It is second only to the highest rank of being an apostle (1 Corinthians 12:28; Ephesians 4:11) and is a gift to be aspired to, for it helps edify believers (1 Corinthians 14:5, 10-12). The words spoken, therefore, should not be treated contemptuously. Paul was not advocating blind acceptance of every word spoken by any self-styled prophet. Instead, believers were to *test everything* against God's words in Scripture, discern what was true and what was false, and then *hold on to the good.* The word translated "good" *(kalos)* was sometimes used for something genuine—for example, a genuine coin as opposed to a counterfeit. All believers are responsible to listen, discern, and learn.

How are believers to test for truth and genuineness? The apostle John explained this in 1 John 4:1-3:

> *Beloved, do not believe every spirit, but test the spirits to see whether they are from God; for many false prophets have gone out into the world. By this you know the Spirit of God: every spirit that confesses that Jesus Christ has come in the flesh is from God, and every spirit that does not confess Jesus is not from God. And this is the spirit of the antichrist, of which you have heard that it is coming; and now it is already in the world.* (NRSV)

> What is Christian perfection? Loving God with all our heart, mind, soul and strength.
> *John Wesley*

Christians should not believe everything they hear just because someone says it is a message inspired by God. There are many ways to test teachers to see if their message is truly from the Lord. One is to check to see if their words match what God says in the Bible. Other tests include their commitment to the body of believers (1 John 2:19), their lifestyle (1 John 3:23-24), and the validity of their message (1 John 4:1-3). The most important test of all is what they believe about Christ.

TEST TIME
We shouldn't make fun of those who don't agree with what we believe ("treat prophecies with contempt"), but we should always "test everything," checking people's words against the Bible, just as the Bereans did in Acts 17:11. We will be on dangerous ground if we scoff at a person who speaks the truth. Instead, we should carefully check out what people say, accepting what is true and rejecting what is false.

However, neither should we believe everything we read or hear. Unfortunately, many ideas printed and taught are not true. Christians should have faith, but we should not be gullible. Verify every message you hear, even if the person who brings it says it's from God. If the message is truly from God, it will be consistent with Christ's teachings.

5:22 Stay away from every kind of evil.^{NLT} The separation is real and important: Believers must "hold on to the good" (5:21) and at the same time *stay away from every kind of evil.* Paul did not mean that believers must literally withdraw from the world, for to do so would mean that they could not shine the light of Christ in order that more might come to him. Christians cannot avoid contact with "every kind of evil" because this world is evil, ruled by the

CHECKLIST FOR ENCOURAGERS

The command to "encourage" others is found throughout the Bible. In 5:11-23, Paul gives many specific examples of how believers can encourage others.

Reference	Example	Suggested Application
5:11	Build each other up.	Point out to someone a quality you appreciate in him or her.
5:12	Respect leaders.	Look for ways to cooperate.
5:13	Hold leaders in highest regard.	Hold back your next critical comment about those in positions of responsibility. Say thank you to your leaders for their efforts.
5:13	Live in peace.	Search for ways to get along with others.
5:14	Warn the idle.	Challenge someone to join you in a worthwhile project.
5:14	Encourage the timid.	Encourage those who are timid by reminding them of God's promises.
5:14	Help the weak.	Support those who are weak by loving them and praying for them.
5:14	Be patient.	Think of a situation that tries your patience, and plan ahead of time how you can stay calm.
5:15	Resist revenge.	Instead of planning to get even with those who mistreat you, do good to them.
5:16	Be joyful.	Remember that even in the midst of turmoil, God is in control.
5:17	Pray continually.	Talk to God—he is always with you.
5:18	Give thanks.	Make a list of all the gifts God has given you, giving thanks to God for each one.
5:19	Do not put out the Spirit's fire.	Cooperate with the Spirit the next time he prompts you to participate in a Christian meeting.
5:20	Do not treat prophecies with contempt.	Receive God's word from those who speak for him.
5:22	Avoid every kind of evil.	Avoid situations where you will be drawn into temptation.
5:23	Count on God's constant help.	Realize that the Christian life is to be lived, not in your own strength, but through God's power.

evil one (see Ephesians 6:12). Believers can, however, make sure
that they don't give evil a foothold by avoiding tempting situations and concentrating on obeying God (see also Romans 12:9).

5:23 **May God himself, the God of peace, sanctify you through and
through. May your whole spirit, soul and body be kept blameless at the coming of our Lord Jesus Christ.**[NIV] The conduct
Paul has been prescribing is impossible from a human standpoint.
People will not naturally rejoice always, pray continually, and give
thanks in every situation (5:16-18), nor can they keep away from
all evil (5:22). But Paul did not expect the Thessalonian believers
to do this in their own strength, so he prayed for them that they
would continue to know the presence of *God himself, the God of
peace,* who would *sanctify [them] through and through.*

Paul described God as "the God of peace" as he often did at
the end of his letters (see Romans 15:33; 16:20; 2 Corinthians
13:11; Philippians 4:9; 2 Thessalonians 3:16). Before his death,
Jesus had told his disciples, "Peace I leave with you; my peace I
give you. I do not give to you as the world gives. Do not let your
hearts be troubled and do not be afraid. . . . I have told you these
things, so that in me you may have peace. In this world you will
have trouble. But take heart! I have overcome the world" (John
14:27; 16:33 NIV). The end result of the Holy Spirit's work in a
believer's life is deep and lasting peace. Unlike worldly peace,
which is usually defined as the absence of conflict, this peace is
confident assurance in any circumstance; with Christ's peace, no
believer needs to fear the present or the future. When the God
of peace moves into a believer's heart and life, he restrains the
hostile forces and offers comfort in place of conflict. One day the
God of peace will come to reign in ultimate and final peace; he
gives his people a taste of that.

As God takes up residence within a believer, he begins the process of "sanctification"—the change that he makes in all believers' lives as they grow in faith. Jesus said, "You are to be perfect,
even as your Father in heaven is perfect" (Matthew 5:48 NLT).
Believers are sanctified (set apart) by the work of Christ. It is ini-
tiated by God's Spirit when they believe. It is a process whereby
believers dedicate themselves to proper living. While perfection
will not occur until believers are in heaven, sanctification is the
process of moving toward that goal, moving toward Christlike-
ness. Believers have been set free from sin's control, but sin is
still an issue during this life. Victories can be claimed every day
in every area of life, however, as God sanctifies. Romans 6–8
describes the process (see also Ephesians 4:13; Colossians 1:28;
2 Thessalonians 2:13; 2 Timothy 2:21; 1 Peter 1:2).

GOD IS FAITHFUL

When thinking of faithfulness, a friend or spouse may come to mind. People who are faithful to us accept and love us, even when we are unlovable. Faithful people keep their promises, whether promises of support or promises made in marriage vows. God's faithfulness is like human faithfulness, only perfect. His love is absolute, and his promises are irrevocable. He loves us in spite of our constant bent toward sin, and he keeps all the promises he has made to us, even when we break our promises to him. Listed below are a few of the verses that describe God's faithfulness (italics added):

Reference	*Verse*
Exodus 34:6	"Yahweh! The LORD! The God of compassion and mercy! I am slow to anger and filled with unfailing love and *faithfulness*" (NLT).
Deuteronomy 7:9	"Know therefore that the LORD your God is God; he is the *faithful* God, keeping his covenant of love to a thousand generations of those who love him and keep his commands" (NIV).
Deuteronomy 32:4	"He is the Rock; his deeds are perfect. Everything he does is just and fair. He is a *faithful* God who does no wrong; how just and upright he is!" (NLT).
Psalm 33:4	"For the word of the LORD is right and true; he is *faithful* in all he does" (NIV).
Psalm 36:5	"Your love, O LORD, reaches to the heavens, your *faithfulness* to the skies" (NIV).
Psalm 89:1-2, 5, 8	"I will sing of the LORD's unfailing love forever! Young and old will hear of your *faithfulness*. Your unfailing love will last forever. Your *faithfulness* is as enduring as the heavens. . . . All heaven will praise your great wonders, LORD; myriads of angels will praise you for your *faithfulness*. . . . O LORD God of Heaven's Armies! Where is there anyone as mighty as you, O LORD? You are entirely *faithful*" (NLT).
Psalm 91:4	"He will cover you with his feathers, and under his wings you will find refuge; his *faithfulness* will be your shield and rampart" (NIV).
Psalm 100:5	For the LORD is good. His unfailing love continues forever, and his *faithfulness* continues to each generation" (NLT).
Psalm 117:2	"For he loves us with unfailing love; the LORD's *faithfulness* endures forever. Praise the LORD!" (NLT).

Psalm 145:13	"Your kingdom is an everlasting kingdom, and your dominion endures through all generations. The LORD is *faithful* to all his promises and loving toward all he has made" (NIV).
Lamentations 3:22-23	"Because of the LORD's great love we are not consumed, for his compassions never fail. They are new every morning; great is your *faithfulness*" (NIV).
1 Corinthians 10:13	"The temptations in your life are no different from what others experience. And God is *faithful*. He will not allow the temptation to be more than you can stand. When you are tempted, he will show you a way out so that you can endure" (NLT).
1 Thessalonians 5:24	"He who calls you is *faithful*, who also will do it" (NKJV).
2 Thessalonians 3:3	"But the Lord is *faithful*, and he will strengthen and protect you from the evil one" (NIV).
Hebrews 10:23	"Let us hold unswervingly to the hope we profess, for he who promised is *faithful*" (NIV).
1 Peter 4:19	"So then, those who suffer according to God's will should commit themselves to their *faithful* Creator and continue to do good" (NIV).
1 John 1:9	"If we confess our sins, He is *faithful* and just to forgive us our sins and to cleanse us from all unrighteousness" (NKJV).
Revelation 19:11	"Then I saw heaven opened, and a white horse was standing there. It's rider was named *Faithful* and True" (NLT).

In order to be sanctified "through and through," God will need to work in all areas of a person's life—the *whole spirit, soul and body.* The spirit, soul, and body refer not so much to the distinct parts of a person as to the entire being of a person. This expression is Paul's way of saying that God must be involved in every aspect of a believer's life. A person's spiritual life cannot be separated from everything else; being a Christian was never meant to be a "Sundays only" proposition. Instead, faith should so permeate each believer's life that his or her whole being is coming more and more under God's loving control. As believers walk with God, though they will still sin, they confess and forgive, seeking daily to draw closer to God who will keep them *blameless* for Christ's return. Perhaps the Thessalonian believers were wondering if believers who died before the Second Coming would be able to receive this perfection from Christ. Paul explained that the supernatural process would occur for all believers. God will preserve his people.

Paul had been discussing the Second Coming (4:13–5:10), so he appropriately ended this prayer with a reference to it. The conclusion of this sanctification process is *the coming of our Lord Jesus Christ,* who will bring his people to complete perfection and take them with him to his kingdom. "But our citizenship is in heaven. And we eagerly await a Savior from there, the Lord Jesus Christ, who, by the power that enables him to bring everything under his control, will transform our lowly bodies so that they will be like his glorious body" (Philippians 3:20-21 NIV).

5:24 **He who calls you is faithful, who also will do it.**^{NKJV} Why could the Thessalonians count on this ongoing sanctification, blame-lessness at Christ's return, and future perfection? Because *he who calls you is faithful, who also will do it.* The promise comes from God himself—the Author of the plan, the One who accomplished it through the death of his Son, the One who *calls* his people, and the One who cannot lie. "God is not a human being, that he should lie, or a mortal, that he should change his mind. Has he promised, and will he not do it? Has he spoken, and will he not fulfill it?" (Numbers 23:19 NRSV).

Faithfulness is a characteristic of God (see the chart "God Is Faithful" on pages 90–91). God created the world, and he has faithfully ordered it and kept it since the Creation. Because God is faithful, believers can count on him to fulfill his promises to them. If God can oversee the forces of nature, surely he can see his people through the trials they face. Trusting in God's faithful-ness day by day gives confidence in his great promises for the future. What he has promised, he *will do.*

5:25 **Beloved, pray for us.**^{NRSV} Paul spent a lot of time in prayer for the believers in the various churches (see the chart "Paul's Prayers" on page16). He mentioned several times his own prayers for the Thessalonians (1:2; 3:10, 12-13; 5:23; 2 Thessalonians 1:11). But Paul also asked believers to pray for him and his fellow missionaries (see also Ephesians 6:19; Colossians 4:3; 2 Thessalonians 3:1). Every believer, even this gifted apostle, needs the prayers of fellow believers.

5:26 **Greet all the brothers and sisters with a holy kiss.**^{NRSV} To *greet all the brothers and sisters with a holy kiss* was encouraged by Paul as a way to greet Christians and a way to help break down the divisions in this church. Kissing was a normal way of greet-ing each other in Paul's day. This "holy kiss," or "kiss of love," expressed the love and unity among the believers. Paul wanted his readers to express their love and unity to one another. Paul used the same expression in Romans 16:16; 1 Corinthians 16:20; and

2 Corinthians 13:12. Peter also recommended the "holy kiss" to the believers (1 Peter 5:14).

THE KISS
Paul encouraged the "holy kiss" as a way for Christians to greet each other and a way to help break down the divisions in this church. This custom was carried over from Jewish society, where a kiss was a normal greeting. Today, a handshake or hug conveys the same warmth, genuineness, and respect. To a church mired in a pattern of divisiveness and personal competitiveness, Paul issued a simple order: Show the world you appreciate each other. Make sure your greetings are heartfelt and enthusiastic.

5:27 I command you in the name of the Lord to read this letter to all the brothers and sisters.^{NLT} Paul's wording here is very strong. "I command you in the name of the Lord" means something like, "I put you on oath before the Lord." Paul did not write merely to the leaders; he wrote to everyone, so *all the Christians* needed to hear every word of it. For every Christian to hear this letter, it had to be read in a public meeting—there were not enough copies to circulate. Paul wanted to make sure that everyone had the opportunity to hear his message because he was answering important questions and offering needed encouragement.

5:28 The grace of our Lord Jesus Christ be with you.^{NRSV} As Paul began this letter (1:1), so he ended it. Paul's final prayer was for *the grace of our Lord Jesus Christ [to] be with [them].* Paul often ended his letters this way, asking his readers to continue to experience God's undeserved kindness and love every day of their lives and then to pass along that grace to others.

CONTINUE IN THE FAITH
The Thessalonian church was young, and its members needed help and encouragement. Both the persecution they faced and the temptations of their pagan culture were potential problems for these new Christians. Paul wrote, therefore, to strengthen their faith and bolster their resistance to persecution and temptation. We, too, have a responsibility to help new believers and to make sure that they continue in their faith and don't become sidetracked by wrong beliefs or practices. First Thessalonians can better equip us to help our brothers and sisters in Christ.

INTRODUCTION TO 2 THESSALONIANS

If you've played "telephone," you know the routine. A message is whispered down the line, person to person; eventually, the last person in line reveals what he or she heard. Usually what the last person reports differs radically from what had been sent by the first person, the message having been distorted in the continued process of listening and repeating.

Communication can be tricky, and what is heard and repeated is not always what was said in the first place.

Evidently, that's what happened in Thessalonica. Paul had written his warm and personal first letter to teach, encourage, and strengthen the believers there. Perhaps the most powerful message of Paul's letter was his teaching about the Second Coming. Paul wanted to comfort those who had lost loved ones and to give all of them hope. Jesus would soon return, and they should be ready.

Like the game of "telephone," however, many of the Thessalonians heard the wrong message. Or they may have received false information from outsiders who, because of ignorance or selfish motives, had twisted the truth. Thinking Paul was stating that Jesus would come at any minute, they stopped working and started watching. The increased persecution of the church made this interpretation of Paul's words more plausible. *Surely this is the Day of the Lord,* many must have thought.

Upon learning of this miscommunication and misunderstanding, Paul wrote quickly, instructing further about the Second Coming and the Day of the Lord.

As you read 2 Thessalonians, think of how the first-century believers in that Greek city must have received Paul's message and how they probably changed their behavior. And consider what you should do to be ready for Christ's return—it's closer now than ever before!

AUTHOR

Paul (Saul of Tarsus): Apostle of Christ, missionary, gifted teacher, and founder of the church at Thessalonica.

Just like 1 Thessalonians, the first verse of 2 Thessalonians mentions Paul, Silas, and Timothy as those who were sending this letter. The contents, however, clearly reveal Paul to be the primary author. For example, he used the pronoun "I" when referring to his preaching: "Don't you remember that I told you about all this when I was with you?" (2:5 NLT). He also used the pronoun "I" when he signed the letter in his own handwriting: "HERE IS MY GREETING IN MY OWN HANDWRITING—PAUL. I DO THIS IN ALL MY LETTERS TO PROVE THEY ARE FROM ME" (3:17 NLT). Paul hoped that his signature on this letter would silence any critics and those skeptical that the letter had actually come from him. For these reasons, Paul's authorship of 2 Thessalonians was widely accepted by the early church. Some of the earliest Christian writers, such as Ignatius, Polycarp, and Justin Martyr, attributed 2 Thessalonians to Paul.

Challenges to Pauline Authorship. Even with this extraordinary amount of evidence, some critical scholars still have questioned Paul's authorship. The objections are usually based on the idea that 1 and 2 Thessalonians teach two contradictory doctrines about Jesus' return. According to these scholars, 1 Thessalonians teaches that Christ's return is imminent; it could occur any day or moment—even tomorrow (1 Thessalonians 5:2-6)! In contrast, 2 Thessalonians explains the delay of Christ's return, that he won't come back until the man of lawlessness has wreaked havoc on the earth (see 2:1-12). Because the descriptions of the Second Coming seem to differ, some scholars believe that 2 Thessalonians was written by someone who disagreed with the way Paul had depicted Christ's return in 1 Thessalonians. And, as the theory goes, this anonymous writer sought to replace 1 Thessalonians with his own version of the letter. That is why the author tells his readers not to accept any other teaching about Christ's return—even if it was supposedly from Paul himself (see 2:2).

It must be said that the two views of the Second Coming do not comprise a contradiction at all. In fact, Jesus' teachings on the end times hold a similar tension. He exhorted his disciples: "So you, too, must keep watch! For you don't know what day your Lord is coming" (Matthew 24:42 NLT). The same passage, however, has Jesus telling his disciples that persecution (Matthew 24:9), false christs (Matthew 24:24), and the abomination in the Holy Place (Matthew 24:15) have to occur first. Now consider what Paul wrote to the Thessalonians. First he exhorted them to be prepared for Christ's imminent return (1 Thessalonians 5:1-4). Upon reading this, many of the Thessalonians became confused, expecting Jesus to return the next hour, day, or week. So in his second letter Paul cleared up the confusion by describing some of the events that would precede the Second Coming (2:1-10). The different emphases of 1 and 2 Thessalonians are not contradictory. Second Thessalonians simply corrects some of the misunderstandings in the church about Christ's return.

DATE AND SETTING

Written from Corinth around A.D. 51, a few months after
1 Thessalonians.

Shortly after writing his first letter to the church at Thessalonica, Paul wrote 2 Thessalonians. He wrote this letter from Corinth also (for more on Corinth, see the introduction to 1 Thessalonians). The content of 2 Thessalonians verifies Corinth as the location.

- Paul, Timothy, and Silas were still together (1:1), and Corinth is the only place the three were known to have gathered after the initial evangelism of Thessalonica (see Acts 18:5).
- The condition of the Thessalonian church was much the same: The believers were still being persecuted (compare 1 Thessalonians 1:6 to 2 Thessalonians 1:4). In spite of its troubles, the Thessalonian church was still growing (compare 1 Thessalonians 1:8 to 2 Thessalonians 1:3).

An Alternative Date for 2 Thessalonians. Although most Bible scholars hold that 2 Thessalonians was written after 1 Thessalonians, some say that 2 Thessalonians was actually written first. These scholars assert that while Paul was in Athens (see Acts 17:13-34) he sent Timothy back to Thessalonica to see how the believers were doing (see 1 Thessalonians 3:2). According to these scholars, Paul gave the letter we call 2 Thessalonians to Timothy at that time. Later, after Timothy returned from this visit, Paul wrote 1 Thessalonians. The argument for this theory hinges on the fact that 1 Thessalonians seems to develop in more detail the themes and issues of 2 Thessalonians—especially the teaching on Christ's return (compare 1 Thessalonians 5:1-11 with 2 Thessalonians 2:1-12).

The primary problem with this theory is that 2 Thessalonians specifically mentions a previous letter, while 1 Thessalonians doesn't: "With all these things in mind, dear brothers and sisters, stand firm and keep a strong grip on everything we taught you both in person and by letter" (2:15). If 2 Thessalonians is the first letter to the Thessalonians, as some critical scholars suppose, then Paul would have had to have written another letter to the Thessalonians. But there is simply no reason to believe that

Paul wrote three letters to the Thessalonians. It is reasonable
to assume, therefore, that 2 Thessalonians was written after
1 Thessalonians.

AUDIENCE

The believers in Thessalonica.

Second Thessalonians was written to the same group of people
to whom 1 Thessalonians was written: the believers in Thessalonica (for more on Thessalonica and the church there, see the
introduction to 1 Thessalonians).

Because of the similarities between the two letters, some critical
scholars have asserted that each letter was sent to a distinct group
in the Thessalonian church: 1 Thessalonians to the Jewish Christians and 2 Thessalonians to the Gentile Christians. This may be a
convenient explanation for the similarities between the two letters,
but the evidence for this theory is meager. Second Thessalonians
addresses no issue that is peculiarly Jewish. Moreover, Paul's
other letters address Jews and Gentiles together, encouraging them
to become one in Christ (see Romans 10:12; Galatians 3:28). It
would have been uncharacteristic of Paul to send two separate
letters—one addressed to the Jewish Christians, the other to the
Gentile Christians. That would have merely promoted more division in the church.

Other scholars have speculated that Paul wrote 2 Thessalonians
to another church nearby that was experiencing persecution, such
as the church at Berea or Philippi. This is total speculation since
no manuscript evidence exists for this theory either. Instead, early
manuscripts include the first verse of 2 Thessalonians, which simply states: "To the church of the Thessalonians" (NIV).

OCCASION AND PURPOSE

To clear up confusion about the second coming of Christ.

After sending his first letter to the church in Thessalonians,
Paul received additional news about the believers there. They
were enduring intense persecution and great hardship (1:4), but
despite their troubles, they were clinging to the faith. Some, however, were claiming that Jesus had already returned (2:1-2). These
believers may have misunderstood Paul's statement that Christ's
return would be as unexpected as a thief coming in the middle of
the night (1 Thessalonians 5:1-3). Or perhaps they had received
another letter, claiming to be from Paul, that simply declared
that Christ had already returned (2:2-3). That rumor, along with
persecution, was disrupting and weakening the young church.

Thinking they were in the final days, some believers were refusing to work (compare 1 Thessalonians 5:14 with 2 Thessalonians 3:11-12).

Paul knew that he had to write a second letter to dispel the rumors and to guide the young church. First he encouraged believers to continue to endure persecution. One day God himself would reward them and punish those who were persecuting them (1:3-12). Second he tried to clear up the confusion about Christ's second coming. He adamantly denied that Jesus had already returned (2:1-2). Believers should not listen to anyone who claimed that he had, for the man of lawlessness had not yet appeared. This man's reign of terror would precede the Second Coming (2:1-12).

Paul also had strong words for those believers who were refusing to work. He had already warned them to stop being lazy (1 Thessalonians 4:11-12; 5:14). This letter takes these lazy ones more seriously. Apparently Paul believed that they were causing trouble because they were gossiping instead of working (3:6, 11). So Paul commanded the believers to stay away from anyone who refused to work after being admonished twice. Those people were simply troublemakers.

In summary, this letter reveals the heart of a concerned pastor. Paul didn't want any false teaching to distract his new converts from the Christian faith. They had already suffered too much for Christ to be sidetracked by idle gossip.

MESSAGE

Persecution; Christ's Return; Great Rebellion; Persistence.

Persecution (1:4-12; 3:1-5). Knowing that believers were being persecuted for their faith, Paul encouraged the church to persevere despite their troubles and trials. He affirmed that God would bring victory to his faithful followers and judge those who persecute them.

Importance for Today. Christians are still being persecuted because of their strong faith in Christ. Some of the persecutions are overt and obvious. But many are subtle and secretive. In both cases, believers need to focus on God and his goodness, love, and call to faithfulness. God has promised to reward faith by giving believers his power and helping them bear persecution. Suffering for the faith will strengthen us to serve Christ. We must be faithful to him.

Christ's return (1:5-7; 2:1-12). Because Paul had written that Christ could return at any moment, some of the Thessalonian believers had stopped working in order to wait for him. Certainly believers should be prepared for the Second Coming. But this preparation includes faithfully fulfilling the work to which God has called them, living upright and moral lives, and using their gifts and talents for God's glory.

Importance for Today. Christ will return and bring total victory to all who trust in him. This truth should give believers hope regardless of their circumstances. It also should motivate believers to make the most of the time they have left on earth, to use their gifts, and to spread the Good News. If we are ready, we need not be concerned about *when* he will return. We should stand firm, keep working, and wait for Christ.

Great Rebellion (2:3-12). Before Christ's return, a great rebellion against God will be led by the man of lawlessness (the Antichrist). God will remove all the restraints on evil before he brings judgment on the rebels. The Antichrist will attempt to deceive many.

Importance for Today. We should not be afraid when we see evil increase. God is in control, no matter how evil the world becomes. God guards us during Satan's attacks. We can have victory over evil by remaining faithful to God.

Persistence (1:4, 11-12; 2:13-17; 3:1-15). Members of the Thessalonian church had quit working and had become disorderly and disobedient. Paul chastised them for their idleness. He called them to show courage and true Christian conduct. He also challenged them to pray for courage and for each other and to stand firm in their faith.

Importance for Today. Believers must never get so tired of doing right that they stop doing it. Instead, we should stand strong in our faith and continue to live the way God wants us to live. We can be persistent by making the most of our time and talent. Our endurance will be rewarded. When do you feel like giving up or giving in? What can you do to ensure your faithfulness to the Lord?

VITAL STATISTICS

Purpose: To clear up the confusion about the second coming of
Christ

Author: Paul

To whom written: The church at Thessalonica and all believers
everywhere

Date written: About A.D. 51 or 52, a few months after
1 Thessalonians, from Corinth

Setting: Many in the church were confused about the timing of
Christ's return. Because of mounting persecution, they thought
the Day of the Lord must be imminent, and they interpreted
Paul's first letter to say that the Second Coming would be at
any moment. In light of this misunderstanding, many persisted
in being idle and disorderly, with the excuse of waiting for
Christ's return.

Key verse: "May the Lord lead your hearts into a full
understanding and expression of the love of God and the
patient endurance that comes from Christ" (3:5 NLT).

Key people: Paul, Silas, Timothy

Key place: Thessalonica

Special features: This is a follow-up letter to 1 Thessalonians. In
this letter, Paul indicates various events that must precede the
second coming of Christ.

OUTLINE

Paul wrote to encourage those who were facing persecution and
to correct a misunderstanding about the timing of Christ's return.
The teaching about the Lord's return had promoted idleness in
this young church. The imminent coming of Christ should never
make us idle; we should be even more busy—living purely, using
our time well, and working for his kingdom. We must work not
only during easy times, when it is convenient, but also during
difficult times. Christians must patiently watch for Christ's return
and work for him while we wait.

1. The bright hope of Christ's return (1:1–2:17)
2. Living in the light of Christ's return (3:1-18)

2 Thessalonians 1

Paul wrote this letter from Corinth less than a year after he wrote
1 Thessalonians. He and his companions, Timothy and Silas, had
visited Thessalonica on Paul's second missionary journey (Acts
17:1-10). They established the church there, but Paul had to leave
suddenly because of persecution. This prompted him to write
his first letter (1 Thessalonians), which contains words of comfort and encouragement. Paul then heard how the Thessalonians
had responded to this letter. The good news was that they were
continuing to grow in their faith. But the bad news was that false
teachings about Christ's return were spreading, leading many to
quit their jobs and wait for the end of the world. So Paul wrote to
the Thessalonians again. While the purpose of Paul's first letter
was to comfort the Thessalonians with the assurance of Christ's
second coming, the purpose of this second letter was to correct
false teaching about the Second Coming.

1:1 Paul, Silas and Timothy.^{NIV} This second letter to the church in
Thessalonica begins just like 1 Thessalonians. Paul was the head
of the missionary team that had brought the gospel to that city. A
well-educated Jew, he started out by persecuting Christians (Acts
8:3) but ended up being caught by Jesus Christ. God had chosen
Paul to take the gospel message to the Gentiles (Acts 9:15).
Paul took three missionary journeys across much of the Roman
Empire, sharing the gospel and planting churches as he went. For
more information on Paul, see the "Author" section of the introduction to this commentary.

Silas is also called Silvanus. He is called a prophet (Acts
15:32), and he was highly regarded in the Jerusalem church. Silas
was on the team that delivered the decision from the Jerusalem
council to the church in Antioch regarding Gentiles and the
Christian faith (Acts 15:22). After Paul and Barnabas (who had
gone on the first missionary journey) parted ways in a disagreement, Paul chose Silas to accompany him on his second missionary journey (Acts 15:40). Silas is mentioned in the salutation of

both letters to the Thessalonians, and he worked with Timothy in Corinth (2 Corinthians 1:19).

Paul and Barnabas met the young man named Timothy in the city of Lystra during their first missionary journey (Acts 16:1-3). When Paul and Silas returned to that city during the second trip, they invited Timothy to join them. Timothy became a great help to Paul, for he not only traveled with Paul but sometimes went out as Paul's emissary. At times Timothy would check on the progress of churches; at other times he would stay in a city to continue teaching while Paul moved on to unevangelized places (see Acts 17:14-15; 18:5; 19:22; 1 Corinthians 4:17; Philippians 2:19; 1 Thessalonians 3:2).

At this point all three of these men (Paul, Silas, and Timothy) were in Corinth (Acts 18:5). A few months earlier, Timothy had gone back to Thessalonica to check on the believers there and had returned to Paul with the good news of their faith (1 Thessalonians 3:5-6). Paul had written 1 Thessalonians to express his great joy as well as to answer some questions. But some time had passed, and Paul had heard about some other problems in Thessalonica: The church was still facing persecution, false teachers were giving wrong information about the Second Coming, and some of the believers had stopped working in order to wait for Christ's return.

To the church of the Thessalonians in God our Father and the Lord Jesus Christ.^{NIV} Thessalonica was the capital and largest city of the Roman province of Macedonia. The most important Roman highway—extending from Rome to the Orient—went through Thessalonica. This highway, along with the city's busy seaport, made Thessalonica one of the wealthiest and most flourishing trade centers in the Roman Empire. Thessalonica was a free city, meaning it was allowed self-rule and was exempted from most of the restrictions placed by Rome on other cities. Because of this open climate, however, the city had many pagan religions and cultural influences that challenged the Christians' faith.

Paul had planted *the church of the Thessalonians* when he and his companions visited Thessalonica on their second missionary journey (Acts 17:1-10). The Greek word for "church" is *ekklesia,* which simply means "an assembly." This assembly of believers was *in God our Father and the Lord Jesus Christ* because the people had come to faith in Christ. God is not the Father only of Jesus Christ, but he is "our" Father as well—the Father of all believers. The phrase "the Lord Jesus Christ" points to Christ's divinity and oneness with the Father.

The Thessalonian believers had strong faith, for despite persecution, they had endured. So strong was their faith, wrote Paul,

that they had become "an example to all the believers in Greece
. . . for wherever we go we find people telling us about your faith
. . . talking about the wonderful welcome you gave us and how
you turned away from idols to serve the true and living God.
And they speak of how you are looking forward to the coming of
God's Son from heaven" (1 Thessalonians 1:7-10 NLT). For more
information on Thessalonica, see the "Audience" section of the
introduction to 1 Thessalonians in this commentary.

**1:2 Grace to you and peace from God our Father and the Lord
Jesus Christ.**^{NKJV} Paul often would begin his letters with a
greeting of *grace* and *peace.* "Grace" is God's unmerited favor
bestowed upon sinful people; "peace" refers to the peace that
Christ made between believers and God through his death on
the cross. By calling God *our Father*
(Greek, *patros*), Paul presented God
as the Father of all believers, shown
by God's sovereign authority and
his loving care for his children. See
Galatians 4:4-7 for more on God's
fatherly love. If God is their Father,
then all Christians form the family of
God. Christians must then treat each
other as true brothers and sisters.
Paul places Jesus Christ side by side
with God as the provider of grace and
peace. Paul calls Jesus *Lord* (Greek,
kyrios), meaning master, one who
deserves our obedience. Christ brings
grace in the form of life's great blessings and the ability to handle difficulties, even persecution; he offers peace
that is an inner calm no matter what
the outward circumstances. Many
early Christians faced persecution—
from minor to severe. Thessalonica
was no exception (1:4). Paul himself
faced it throughout his ministry; he
had even been driven out of Thessa-
lonica (Acts 17:5-10). That the young Thessalonian church could
experience God's grace and peace through any trial strengthened
their faith, gave them great hope, and made them an example to
the rest of the believers in other cities across the empire.

> This idea of spiritual
> growth is foreign to
> many people, not least
> in the areas of faith and
> love. We tend to speak
> of faith in static terms
> as something we either
> have or have not. "I
> wish I had your faith,"
> we say, like, "I wish I
> had your complexion,"
> as if it were a genetic
> endowment. Or we
> complain, "I've lost my
> faith," like, "I've lost my
> spectacles," as if it
> were a commodity. But
> faith is a relationship of
> trust in God, and like all
> relationships is a living,
> dynamic, growing
> thing.   *John Stott*

**1:3 Dear brothers and sisters, we can't help but thank God for
you, because your faith is flourishing and your love for one**

THEOLOGY OF TRIALS IN THE NEW TESTAMENT

As we live for Christ, we will experience troubles because we are trying to be God's people in a perverse world. Some people say that troubles are the result of sin or lack of faith, but the Bible teaches that they may be a part of God's plan for believers. Our problems can help us look upward and forward, instead of inward; they can build strong character; and they can provide us with opportunities to comfort others who are also struggling. Your troubles may be an indication that you are taking a stand for Christ.

Suffering is not always the result of sin.	John 9:2-3, "His disciples asked him, 'Rabbi, who sinned, this man or his parents, that he was born blind?' 'Neither this man nor his parents sinned,' said Jesus, 'but this happened so that the work of God might be displayed in his life'" (NIV).
God provides hope and love in suffering.	Romans 5:3-5, "We also rejoice in our sufferings, because we know that suffering produces perseverance; perseverance, character; and character, hope. And hope does not disappoint us, because God has poured out his love into our hearts by the Holy Spirit, whom he has given us" (NIV).
Problems help us trust in God's sovereign purpose for our lives.	Romans 8:28-29, "We know that all things work together for good for those who love God, who are called according to his purpose. For those whom he foreknew he also predestined to be conformed to the image of his Son, in order that he might be the first-born within a large family" (NRSV).
Suffering enables us to comfort others.	2 Corinthians 1:3-5, "Praise be to the God and Father of our Lord Jesus Christ, the Father of compassion and the God of all comfort, who comforts us in all our troubles, so that we can comfort those in any trouble with the comfort we ourselves have received from God. For just as the sufferings of Christ flow over into our lives, so also through Christ our comfort overflows" (NIV).
Our eternal reward outweighs our suffering.	2 Corinthians 4:17-18, "For this slight momentary affliction is preparing us for an eternal weight of glory beyond all measure, because we look not at what can be seen but at what cannot be seen; for what can be seen is temporary, but what cannot be seen is eternal" (NRSV).

Problems may be a confirmation that we are living for Christ.	2 Thessalonians 1:5, "This is evidence of the righteous judgment of God, and is intended to make you worthy of the kingdom of God, for which you are also suffering" (NRSV).
Trials help train us to be more fruitful.	Hebrews 12:11, "No discipline seems pleasant at the time, but painful. Later on, however, it produces a harvest of righteousness and peace for those who have been trained by it" (NIV).
Problems help us mature.	James 1:2-4, "My brothers and sisters, whenever you face trials of any kind, consider it nothing but joy, because you know that the testing of your faith produces endurance; and let endurance have its full effect, so that you may be mature and complete, lacking in nothing" (NRSV).
When we suffer, we share in the suffering of Christ.	1 Peter 4:12-14, "Dear friends, do not be surprised at the painful trial you are suffering, as though something strange were happening to you. But rejoice that you participate in the sufferings of Christ, so that you may be overjoyed when his glory is revealed. If you are insulted because of the name of Christ, you are blessed, for the Spirit of glory and of God rests on you" (NIV).

another is growing.[NLT] Regardless of the contents of Paul's letters, his style was affirming. Paul began most of his letters by stating what he most appreciated about his readers and the joy he felt because of their faith in God. In 1 Thessalonians, Paul had commended the Thessalonians for their faith, love, and hope (1 Thessalonians 1:3). This verse commends their faith and love; the next verse, their hope.

Paul had prayed that the Thessalonians' faith would deepen and that their love would grow and overflow (1 Thessalonians 3:10, 12; 4:10). In the months since he had last written them, Paul could see that their faith was *flourishing* and that their *love for one another [was] growing.* Paul chose colorful words to describe this growth. The word translated "flourishing" *(hyperauxenei)* is used only here in the New Testament and speaks of the type of growth a healthy plant makes. The picture is of internal growth, like that of an oak tree. The word translated "growing" *(pleonazei)* is also a strong verb picturing something that spreads out or disperses widely—like floodwaters. The Thessalonians' internal faith was flourishing like a healthy plant; their external love was spreading out to many (see also 1 Thessalonians 3:12).

That was quite a testament to the faith of these believers, considering the persecution they continued to endure (1:4; 1 Thessalonians 1:6). No wonder Paul *always* thanked God in his prayers for these believers, knowing that such thanksgiving was *right*. Paul was not flattering them; the praise he gave them, both in the first letter (1 Thessalonians 1:4-10) and here, was sincere. God had truly been working in these believers' lives.

GROWING LOVE

The Thessalonians were growing in their love. Too often we think of love as either on or off, all or nothing. Paul tells us that we can nurture and grow love. True love is not static; it reaches out and draws others in. God loves us so much that he sent his Son to die in our place. When we talk to people about Christ, our love must be like his—we must willingly give up our own comfort and security so that others might receive God's love. We can grow in love by not limiting our contact to those of our own race, nation, or community. Are there people or groups that, by your attitude or behavior, you are brushing aside? Take a step to grow in love and reach out to others.

1:4 **We proudly tell God's other churches about your endurance and faithfulness in all the persecutions and hardships you are suffering.**[NLT] In 1:3 Paul commends the believers' faith and love; here he commends their hope as he speaks of their *endurance.* In 1 Thessalonians 1:3, where Paul also commended their faith, love, and hope (or anticipation), he referred to the believers' hope as being inspired by "endurance." Thus, Paul did not in this letter skip "hope" as if he could not commend them this time; instead, their endurance proved that their hope was strong and secure.

Persevering in difficulty would be worth little without faith and love as the motivators. So after Paul commended their faith and love in 1:3, he wrote, *We proudly tell God's other churches about your endurance and faithfulness in all the persecutions and hardships you are suffering.* Some translations use the word "boast" for "we proudly tell." Apparently it was not Paul's pattern to "proudly tell God's other churches" about one group of believers in order to boast about certain characteristics—certainly a wise decision. In the case of the Thessalonians, however, Paul sang their praises, just as others had already been doing (1 Thessalonians 1:7-10).

The word *hypomone,* translated "endurance," is the same word used in 1 Thessalonians 1:3. It pictures not passive acceptance in the face of difficulty but active strength against it, exhibited by *faithfulness.* The Thessalonian believers remained faithful to

God. The word *diogmois,* "persecutions," refers to assaults made on the believers because of their faith in Christ; *thlipsesin,* "hardships," is a more general word for difficulties in life (pressures or burdens).

Paul had been persecuted during his first visit to Thessalonica (Acts 17:5-9). No doubt those who had responded to his message and had become Christians were continuing to face "persecutions and hardships" caused by both Jews and Gentiles. The present tense, "you are suffering," points out that Paul was speaking of present realities.

In Paul's first letter to the Thessalonians, he wrote that Christ's return would bring deliverance from persecution, and judgment on the persecutors. But this caused the people to expect Christ's return right away to rescue and vindicate them. So Paul had to point out that while waiting for God's kingdom, believers could and should learn endurance and faithfulness from their suffering.

1:5 All this is evidence that God's judgment is right, and as a result you will be counted worthy of the kingdom of God, for which you are suffering.[NIV] How is *all this*—that is, the Thessalonians' endurance and faithfulness in persecution and suffering—*evidence that God's judgment is right?* The word "judgment" should be understood as God's righteous decision to allow suffering in this world to sanctify his people. God has chosen to build his people's character through the difficulties they experience during their lives in this evil world.

Persecution and suffering are unavoidable for those who want to follow Jesus, for Jesus said, "Since [the unbelievers] persecuted me, naturally they will persecute you. . . . They will do all this to you because of me, for they have rejected the one who sent me" (John 15:20-21 NLT). Paul understood that believers would "suffer many hardships to enter the Kingdom of God" (Acts 14:22 NLT) and that "if we are to share his glory, we must also share his suffering" (Romans 8:17 NLT). Therefore, the fact that the Thessalonians were being allowed to suffer for their faith and the fact that in doing so their faith, love, and hope were increasing and strengthening (1:3-4) were *evidence that God's judgment [was] right.* Through suffering, God's people are strengthened. In suffering, they can remember that they *will be counted worthy of the kingdom of God, for which [they] are suffering.* Suffering is not a prerequisite to salvation, not something to do in order to receive salvation. But suffering and faithfulness through suffering show God's work in believers' lives and thus their worthiness for his kingdom. Those willing to suffer for their faith will indeed be *counted,* or "declared," worthy. The suffering believers in

Thessalonica could know that their difficulties were only preparing them for future glory.

COUNTED WORTHY
As we live for Christ, we will experience troubles because we are trying to be God's people in a perverse world. Some people say that troubles are the result of sin or lack of faith, but Paul teaches that they may be a part of God's plan for believers. Our problems can

- help us look upward and forward instead of inward (Mark 13:35-36; Philippians 3:13-14);
- build strong character (Romans 5:3-4);
- provide us with opportunities to comfort others who also are struggling (2 Corinthians 1:3-5);
- test our faith, develop perseverance, and help us become more mature and complete (James 1:2-4).

Your troubles may be an indication that you are taking a stand for Christ. The keys to surviving persecution and trials are endurance and faithfulness. When we are faced with crushing troubles, we can trust that God is using our trials for our good and for his glory. Knowing that God is fair and just will develop patience because we know that he has not forgotten us. In his perfect timing, God will relieve our suffering and punish those who persecute us. Can you trust God even in the midst of suffering?

1:6-7 God is just: He will pay back trouble to those who trouble you and give relief to you who are troubled, and to us as well. This will happen when the Lord Jesus is revealed from heaven in blazing fire with his powerful angels.^{NIV} Not only do sufferings strengthen believers, making them ready for Christ's kingdom, sufferings also set up the perpetrators for punishment. *God is just*—his very nature is justice (see Deuteronomy 32:4; 2 Chronicles 19:7). God will act with complete justice when he punishes sinners, but only after providing a way for people *not* to be punished. He sent his Son to die and take the punishment that sin deserved: "For God so loved the world that He gave His only begotten Son, that whoever believes in Him should not perish but have everlasting life" (John 3:16 NKJV). Only those who accept that sacrifice on their behalf will be saved, however: "Anyone who believes in God's Son has eternal life" (John 3:36 NLT).

Those who accept Christ's sacrifice and align themselves with God find themselves at odds with the evil world. Persecution and suffering have been the lot of many Christians throughout the ages. One day, however, God *will pay back trouble to those who trouble* his people. Justice will be served; God will see to it that those who inflicted persecution and suffering will themselves receive much worse. "Anyone who doesn't obey the Son will never experience eternal life but remains under God's angry judgment" (John 3:36 NLT). Not only will God punish evildoers, but he will also *give relief to you who are troubled, and to us as well* (see Revelation 6:9-11, where martyrs receive their reward). Paul placed himself and his companions along with the Thessalonian believers as people who needed "relief" from God. There are two dimensions of this "relief." Believers can gain relief from knowing that their sufferings are strengthening them, making them ready for Christ's kingdom (1:5). They can also gain relief from the fact that one day everyone will stand before God; at that time, wrongs will be righted, judgment will be pronounced, and evil will be terminated.

So when will this happen? While those enduring suffering would wish for a quick judgment, it may be that the payback does not occur in this life. But *this will happen* for sure *when the Lord Jesus is revealed from heaven in blazing fire with his powerful angels.* The Lord Jesus "will descend from heaven with a shout, with the voice of an archangel, and with the trumpet of God" (1 Thessalonians 4:16 NKJV; see also commentary there). The word translated "revealed" (or "revelation") is *apokalypsis,* literally meaning "unveiling." Jesus has been to earth before, and he will one day return—this will be his "second coming." In the meantime he has been hidden from view in heaven with God. But on that great day, Christ will be "revealed" to all mankind. The "blazing fire" is a picture of God's holy presence (see Exodus 13:21; Deuteronomy 4:12, 24; Isaiah 66:15; Revelation 1:13-14), and the "powerful angels" are also described in Matthew 25:31; 1 Thessalonians 3:13; Revelation 5:11; 12:7. Christ's return will be unmistakable. His arrival will signal the end of all injustice, retribution against those who have persecuted believers, and the beginning of his holy kingdom.

> We are tempted to inveigh against God and against the miscarriage of justice. "Why doesn't God do something?" we complain indignantly. And the answer is that he *is* doing something and will go on doing it. He is allowing his people to suffer in order to qualify them for his heavenly kingdom. He is allowing the wicked to triumph temporarily, but his just judgment will fall upon them in the end.
>
> *John Stott*

PAYBACK
Paul promised that God would relieve believers and judge those who oppressed them. Dwelling on our troubles may cripple our faith because relief from our human predicament may seem far away. But we must focus on Christ's mercy toward us and his final judgment on all people. God's relief doesn't always come the moment we want it, but God knows the best time to act. When you feel as though God has forgotten you in your troubles, remember that he has set a day for restoring justice.

1:8 **He will punish those who do not know God and do not obey the gospel of our Lord Jesus.**^{NIV} When the Lord Jesus returns, *he will punish.* The act of punishment belongs to God alone; he will deliver the vengeance that sinners deserve. Deuteronomy 32:35 says: "It is mine to avenge; I will repay. In due time their foot will slip; their day of disaster is near and their doom rushes upon them" (NIV). Who will he punish? *Those who do not know God and do not obey the gospel of our Lord Jesus.* Some commentators have interpreted these two phrases to focus on Gentiles first ("those who do not know God") and then Jews (those who "do not obey the gospel of our Lord Jesus"). But Paul probably was not thinking of this because John 8:54-55 describes Jews as not knowing God, and Romans 11:30 describes Gentiles as disobedient to God. More likely, these two phrases are parallel and describe all unbelievers—their willful rejection of God and of the gospel message.

1:9-10 **They will be punished with everlasting destruction and shut out from the presence of the Lord and from the majesty of his power on the day he comes to be glorified in his holy people and to be marveled at among all those who have believed. This includes you, because you believed our testimony to you.**^{NIV} Paul has explained who will be punished and when; this passage explains what that judgment will be: *They will be punished with everlasting destruction and shut out from the presence of the Lord.* The word "punished" pictures those who are rebellious to God receiving their just deserts. At Christ's return, there will be only two groups of people: those who belong to him and those who do not. Jesus told a parable about this in Matthew 25:31-46. Those who belong to Jesus will enter into his everlasting kingdom; those who do not will face "everlasting destruction," described in Revelation as the lake of fire. The scene is described in Revelation 20:11-15:

And I saw a great white throne and the one sitting on it. The earth and sky fled from his presence, but they found no place to hide. I saw the dead, both great and small, standing before God's throne. And the books were opened, including the Book of Life. And the dead were judged according to what they had done, as recorded in the books. The sea gave up its dead, and death and the grave gave up their dead. And all were judged according to their deeds. Then death and the grave were thrown into the lake of fire. This lake of fire is the second death. And anyone whose name was not found recorded in the Book of Life was thrown into the lake of fire. (NLT)

Revelation describes "books" being opened, books that represent God's judgment. These books contain the deeds of everyone, good or evil. People are not saved by deeds, but deeds are seen as clear evidence of a person's actual relationship with God. The Book of Life contains the names of those who have put their trust in Christ to save them. All whose names are not recorded in the Book of Life have not placed their faith in Jesus Christ. There are no gray areas in God's judgment. Those who have not identified with Christ and confessed him as Lord will have no hope, no second chance, no other appeal (see 1 Thessalonians 5:3). To be "punished with everlasting destruction" means to be eternally separated from God—being *shut out* from his presence. This will be the ultimate punishment. "Shut out from his presence" implies not obliteration or total destruction but a conscious, everlasting life of punishment that is the opposite of what believers face (see Matthew 25:41-46). The unbelievers will be banned or excluded from the presence of God, who is the Source of life.

The believers, persecuted and weak as they may be, however, have the Lord and *the majesty of his power* on their side. The power of the oppressors is meaningless when compared to the mighty power of God. For those oppressors, the Lord's *presence* and the "majesty of his power" will be terrifying.

On the day he comes, Christ will *be glorified in his holy people and . . . marveled at among all those who have believed.* The day of grief for the rebellious will be a day of celebration for believers. Jesus Christ will return in "blazing fire" (1:7 NIV); then he will *be glorified in his holy people.* He will impart to his people—those alive and those who have died (1 Thessalonians 4:16-17)—his glory. First Corinthians describes believers' resurrection bodies: "Our bodies are buried in brokenness, but they will be raised in glory. They are buried in weakness, but they will be raised in strength" (1 Corinthians 15:43 NLT). Believers will see Christ's glory, and they will share it. "Dear friends, now we are children of God, and what we will be has not yet been made known. But we know that when he appears, we shall be like him, for we shall see him as he is" (1 John 3:2 NIV).

This glorious promise *includes you,* wrote Paul to the Thessalonian believers, and it includes everyone across the ages who has *believed [the] testimony*—the message of salvation in Jesus Christ.

GOOD WORK!
Paul prayed that the Thessalonian believers would have God's power to carry out God's will and that their faith would result in good work. God's power produces the fruit of goodness in us, resulting in unselfish acts of service toward others. Paul understood good works as faithful service, acts of charity, and involvement in civil affairs. While good works can't save us or even increase God's love for us, they are true indications of our faith and love for Christ. Paul did not make this aspect of discipleship optional. Service to others is a requirement. Everyone who is a Christian should be involved. Does your church encourage everyone's involvement and service? What can your church do to help every member identify the good works that he or she should be doing?

1:11 So we keep on praying for you, asking our God to enable you to live a life worthy of his call. May he give you the power to accomplish all the good things your faith prompts you to do.NLT Paul and his fellow missionaries kept on praying for the Thessalonian believers, just as Paul prayed for all the churches. Although the promise of future glory is sure, believers still have a battle here on earth and need constant prayer from fellow believers. What were Paul and his fellow missionaries praying for? First, that *God* would *enable you to live a life worthy of his call.* To be made "worthy" has the same meaning here as it did in 1:5. Salvation is sure, but the prospect of the glorious future should be an incentive to holy living—and believers will need one another's support and prayers as they seek to live out their faith. The "call" from God is that his people become like Christ (see Romans 8:29). This call is a gradual, lifelong process that will be completed when we see Christ face-to-face (see 1 John 3:2). To be worthy of this call means to want to do what is right and good (as Christ would). Paul wrote to the church in Ephesus, "I therefore, the prisoner in the Lord, beg you to lead a life worthy of the calling to which you have been called" (Ephesians 4:1 NRSV). God has chosen his people to be Christ's representatives on earth, living worthy of the calling they have received—the awesome privilege of being called Christ's very own.

Second, they were praying that God would *give you the power to accomplish all the good things your faith prompts you to do.* Philippians 2:13 says, "For it is God who works in you to will and to act according to his good purpose" (NIV).

1:12 So that the name of our Lord Jesus may be glorified in you, and you in him, according to the grace of our God and the Lord Jesus Christ.^{NRSV} Paul wanted the Thessalonians to show, by God's power, such qualities of character, such good purposes, and acts of faith (1:11), *that the name of [the] Lord Jesus [would] be glorified in [them], and [them] in him.* The ultimate goal of all believers ought to be to glorify Christ through their actions, words, thoughts, and motives. When believers live to glorify Christ, Christ is glorified in them.

Before his death on the cross, Jesus prayed, "Father, the time has come. Glorify your Son, that your Son may glorify you" (John 17:1 NIV). God would glorify his Son through the Crucifixion and Resurrection, and the Son, in turn, would glorify the Father by giving eternal life to the believers.

This can only happen *according to the grace of our God and the Lord Jesus Christ.* Believers cannot show Christ's glory or be glorified in him because of anything they do—it is only because of God's grace. Only by God's grace did Jesus come to die for sinners; only by God's grace can people receive his sacrifice and be saved from their sins.

2 Thessalonians 2

When Paul first wrote to the Thessalonians, they were in danger of losing hope in the Second Coming. Then they shifted to the opposite extreme—some of them thought that Jesus would return at any minute. Paul tried to restore the balance by describing certain events that would occur before Christ's return.

After the introductory prayer (1:11-12) is the main body of this letter. It seems that some of the Thessalonian believers had latched onto wrong teaching regarding Christ's second coming (2:1-3) and what would happen in the world before he returned. Paul had already taught them much when he was with them and had explained more in his first letter (1 Thessalonians 4–5). This letter tells of a time of great rebellion against God led by a man of lawlessness (the Antichrist). God will remove all the restraints on evil before he brings his final judgment.

2:1-2 Concerning the coming of our Lord Jesus Christ and our being gathered to him, we ask you, brothers, not to become easily unsettled or alarmed by some prophecy, report or letter supposed to have come from us, saying that the day of the Lord has already come.^{NIV} This introduces the main topic of this letter and Paul's reason for writing to these *brothers* in the faith in Thessalonica. He had already taught them *concerning the coming of our Lord Jesus Christ and our being gathered to him.* Paul's first letter answered questions regarding the believers who had died, for there was concern that they had missed out on heaven. Another concern was that the expectation of Christ's return was causing some to stop working and just to wait. So Paul's first letter explained that Jesus would come suddenly (1 Thessalonians 5:1-4) and that believers who had already died would rise out of their graves to meet him while those on earth would be "caught up in the clouds to meet the Lord in the air" (1 Thessalonians 4:17 NLT). In 2:1 Paul states that believers will be "gathered to him." Paul used *episynagogue,* a word also used in Hebrews 10:25, where it refers to an assembly "meeting" for worship.

TROUBLE IN THE CHURCH

The second letter to the Thessalonians mentions three groups of people who were troubling the church in Thessalonica:

Persecutors	2 Thessalonians 1:4-10
	(see also 1 Thessalonians 1:6; 2:14; 3:3)
False teachers	2 Thessalonians 2:2-3
Lazy people (loafers)	2 Thessalonians 3:6-15
	(see also 1 Thessalonians 5:14)

Jesus also expressed his desire to "gather" his people (Matthew 23:37; Luke 13:34).

Apparently Paul had heard further questions from these believers, so he added more details about what would happen at Christ's second coming. Also, he knew that persecution was taking its toll on the believers, spiritually and physically (see 1 Thessalonians 1:6; 2 Thessalonians 1:4-7).

BE READY
Before Christ's second coming there will be great suffering and trouble. Evil will not prevail, however, because Christ will return to judge all people. The emphasis, like Jesus' teaching (see Mark 13), is the need for each person to prepare for Christ's return by living right day by day. If we are ready, we won't have to be concerned about the preceding events or the timing of Christ's return because God controls all the events. If we are prepared, we can rest in God's control.

Verse 2 describes a supposed prophecy, one of the false teachings about Christ's second coming. Some were saying *that the day of the Lord has already come.* "Day of the Lord," a common phrase in the Old Testament, refers to some extraordinary happening, whether a present event, an event in the near future, or the final period of history when God will defeat all the forces of evil (see, for example, Isaiah 13:6, 9; Ezekiel 30:3; Amos 5:18, 20; Obadiah 1:15; Zephaniah 1:7, 14; Zechariah 14:1; Malachi 4:5). The description always pictures great suffering and punishment for sinners. In the book of Joel, for example, the phrase "day of the LORD" refers to a time of destruction to come upon the nation of Judah for its sin (Joel 1:15; 2:1, 11, 31; 3:14).

> Loyalty to apostolic teaching, now permanently enshrined in the New Testament, is still the test of truth and the shield against error. *John Stott*

GREAT REBELLION

The New Testament warns about this time of great rebellion (verses quoted from NLT):

Matthew 24:10-12	"Many will turn away from me. . . . Many false prophets will appear. . . . Sin will be rampant everywhere, and the love of many will grow cold."
John 15:21-22	"They will do all this to you because of me, for they have rejected the one who sent me. . . . But now they have no excuse for their sin."
1 Timothy 4:1	"In the last times some will turn away . . . they will follow deceptive spirits and teachings that come from demons."
2 Timothy 3:1-5	"In the last days there will be very difficult times. For people will love only themselves and their money. They will be boastful and proud, scoffing at God. . . . They will consider nothing sacred. . . . They will act religious, but they will reject the power that could make them godly."
2 Peter 3:3-4	"In the last days scoffers will come, mocking the truth and following their own desires. They will say, 'What happened to the promise that Jesus is coming again?'"
Jude 1:18-19	"In the last times there would be scoffers whose purpose in life is to satisfy their ungodly desires. . . . They follow their natural instincts because they do not have God's Spirit living in them."
Revelation 3:10	"Because you have obeyed my command to persevere, I will protect you from the great time of testing that will come upon the whole world to test those who belong to this world."

Even when the "day of the Lord" refers to a present event, it always foreshadows the final Day of the Lord, to which this verse refers. This final event of history has two aspects to it: (1) the Last Judgment on all evil and sin; (2) the final reward for faithful believers. At that time God will intervene directly and dramatically in world affairs. Righteousness and truth will prevail, and Christ will judge sin and set up his eternal kingdom. First there will be much suffering, however, for evil will crescendo as the end draws near. Looking toward this final day, those who trust in the Lord should have hope because all who are faithful will be united forever with God.

False teachers were saying that Judgment Day had come. This

caused many believers to wait expectantly for vindication and relief from suffering. These false teachers had claimed to have had *some prophecy, report or letter* from Paul and his companions apparently stating what the false teachers were teaching. Perhaps a letter, falsely attributed to Paul or his companions, had been sent or some prophecy or sermon had been given that taught that God's kingdom had already arrived. Some have even proposed that the Thessalonians had misunderstood a teaching in one of Paul's letters—a letter that no longer exists. Paul does not identify the source of this false teaching any further, so we do not know.

But when Christ didn't come, when suffering continued or intensified, the believers were becoming *unsettled* and *alarmed.* These words picture unsettled minds and a continuing state of anxiety. The believers certainly wondered if they had somehow missed out or if they were not going to be saved. Paul assured them that they should not be worried by these false teachers and should listen to him instead. Paul's authority as an apostle and their relationship of trust with him should remind them that any teaching that contradicted what he had given them from the Lord would need to be questioned. Paul would not write a letter to a group of such teachers and tell them to spread the message—Paul had shown that he would answer the Thessalonians' questions directly himself or send one of his co-workers. (At the end of this letter, Paul would sign with his own hand to authenticate this document.)

Paul simply wrote that the Day of the Lord had not yet come; three other events would have to happen first: (1) The rebellion must occur (2:3); (2) the man of lawlessness must be revealed (2:3); (3) the restraint of lawlessness must be removed (2:7).

2:3 Don't let anyone deceive you in any way, for that day will not come until the rebellion occurs and the man of lawlessness is revealed, the man doomed to destruction.[NIV] The coming of the Lord will be "like a thief in the night" (1 Thessalonians 5:2 NLT); even so, certain events will precede it. The final Day of the Lord *will not come until the rebellion occurs and the man of lawlessness is revealed.* This "rebellion" will be a massive revolt against God. It may begin among those who believe in God and spread through all people who refuse to accept Christ. Thus it will include Jews who abandon God and some members of the church whose faith is nominal. The word for "rebellion" *(apostasia)* can mean "departure." So some have interpreted this rebellion, or apostasy, to be the Rapture, but the Rapture is "being caught up" or "a gathering," not a departure. So the word refers to abandoning God or deserting one's faith in him. While rebellion against God seems widespread even today, as the coming of Christ nears, this apostasy and active opposition against God will intensify.

During the rebellion, a remarkable man will come into public view. He will have considerable power from Satan and will personify evil. Throughout history certain individuals have epitomized evil and been hostile to everything Christ stands for (see 1 John 2:18; 4:3; 2 John 1:7). Certain Roman emperors fell into that category. The preface to the original King James Version of the Bible named the pope as the "Man of Sin." Hitler and Stalin have been named as well. These "antichrists" have lived in every generation, and others like them will continue to work their evil. Then, just before Christ's second coming, *the man of lawlessness,* a completely evil man, will arise. He will be Satan's tool, equipped with Satan's power (2:9). This man will oppose all law, both God's moral laws or absolutes as well as civil laws. Thus he will promote immorality and anarchy. Jesus warned, "And because of the increase of lawlessness, the love of many will grow cold" (Matthew 24:12 NRSV). This "lawless" man will be *the* Antichrist. He will be in the world, but then he will rise to power and notoriety, shown by the word "revealed." The book of Revelation speaks of a "beast," symbolizing the Antichrist. Revelation 13:5-8 describes him:

> *Then the beast was allowed to speak great blasphemies against God. And he was given authority to do whatever he wanted for forty-two months. And he spoke terrible words of blasphemy against God, slandering his name and his dwelling—that is, those who dwell in heaven. And the beast was allowed to wage war against God's holy people and to conquer them. And he was given authority to rule over every tribe and people and language and nation. And all the people who belong to this world worshiped the beast. They are the ones whose names were not written in the Book of Life.* (NLT)

The beast symbolizes the Antichrist—not Satan, but someone under Satan's power and control (see also Revelation 16:13 and 19:20, where he is the second member of the false trinity). Satan's evil will culminate in a final Antichrist, a man who will focus all the powers of evil against Jesus Christ and his followers. Yet even this man, for all the power that he will attain, is ultimately *doomed to destruction.* (See John 17:12, where Judas is called "the one headed for destruction.") Revelation 20:10 describes it: "Then the devil . . . was thrown into the fiery lake of burning sulfur, joining the beast. . . . There they will be tormented day and night forever and ever" (NLT).

God still reigns, and his victory is certain. The evil man will be destroyed but not before God uses him. Although this man will be Satan's tool, God will still have everything under control, and events will proceed just as he has planned. During this time of great rebellion, the full extent of wickedness will be demonstrated and rebellion against God will be shown in all its horror and ugliness. Always, through all suffering throughout the ages, God is drawing people to himself, calling them to repent and turn to him. This will continue during those last days.

GOD IS IN CONTROL
It is dangerous to label any person, group, or nation as the Antichrist or to try to predict the timing of Christ's return based on that assumption. Paul mentions the Antichrist not so we will try to identify that person specifically but so we might be ready for anything that threatens our faith or unity. If our faith is strong, we don't need to be afraid of what lies ahead because we know that this lawless person or being has already been defeated by God, no matter how powerful he becomes or how terrible our situation seems. God is in control, and he will be victorious over the Antichrist. Our task is to be prepared for Christ's return and to spread the gospel so that even more people will also be prepared.

2:4 **He will oppose and will exalt himself over everything that is called God or is worshiped, so that he sets himself up in God's temple, proclaiming himself to be God.**[NIV] As noted above, the book of Revelation prophesies that "all the people who belong to this world [will worship] the beast" (Revelation 13:8 NLT). In order to be worshiped, this man of lawlessness *will oppose and will exalt himself over everything that is called God or is worshiped.* This man will attempt, and even will seem to be able, to dethrone God and anything else that is worshiped (idols, nature, self) and then will demand worship and obedience to himself alone. The phrase "sets himself up in God's temple" should not be taken literally; instead, it pictures one who proclaims *himself to be God* and then takes God's place of residence and rule, claiming it for his own. Many have claimed such power throughout history (Roman rulers, various political leaders), and many have been pointed out by others as being the Antichrist, but this one human, yet to come, will be the final, decisive personification of lawlessness, evil, and rebellion against God. This one man will precede Christ's return.

This description of the man of lawlessness is similar to the description of Antiochus Epiphanes mentioned in Daniel 11:36-37; he was responsible for the first "abomination of desolation." In 168 B.C. Antiochus Epiphanes sacrificed a pig to Zeus on the sacred temple altar. This abominable act caused the temple to be abandoned (left desolate).

The second fulfillment occurred when Jesus' prediction of the destruction of the temple (Mark 13:2) came true. In A.D. 70, the Roman army destroyed Jerusalem and desecrated the temple.

Some scholars say that a third fulfillment is yet to come. This "abomination of desolation" may look far forward to the end times and to the Antichrist. In the end times the Antichrist will commit the ultimate sacrilege by setting *himself up in God's temple* (perhaps having a statue erected) and ordering everyone to worship him. (See also Revelation 13:14-15.)

2:5 **Do you not remember that I told you these things when I was still with you?**[NRSV] Paul had started the church in Thessalonica and had helped the believers grow into a strong unit that was able to withstand persecution (Acts 17:1-4; 1 Thessalonians 1:6). Apparently he had taught them about the second coming of Christ and the end times. He reminded them, *Do you not remember that I told you these things when I was still with you?* Either they had forgotten his teaching, or the false teachers had been confusing them.

2:6-7 **And now you know what is holding him back, so that he may be revealed at the proper time. For the secret power of lawlessness is already at work; but the one who now holds it back will continue to do so till he is taken out of the way.**[NIV] In the present world—the world of the Thessalonians and the world today—two events are happening simultaneously. First, *the secret power of lawlessness is already at work* although it may not be clearly seen for what it is. The work that the Antichrist, the man of lawlessness, will do is already going on. "Secret" means something hidden, behind the scenes, but something God will reveal. "Lawlessness" is the hidden, subtle, underlying force from which all sin springs. Second, even though this power is working, so is the one who is restraining it. Civilization still has a modicum of decency through law enforcement, education, science, and reason. Although we are horrified by criminal acts, the world has yet to see the real horror of complete lawlessness. This will happen when *the one who now holds it back . . . is taken out of the way.*

Who "holds back" the man of lawlessness? It seems that the Thessalonians knew that answer *(now you know what is holding him back)* from Paul's previous teaching. So Paul referred to it here but did not repeat it. Commentators have considered three possibilities for the identity of this "restrainer": (1) government and law, which help to curb evil; (2) the ministry and activity of the church and the effects of the gospel; (3) the Holy Spirit. The Bible is not clear on the identity of this restrainer, only that he will not restrain forever. Then the man of lawlessness will be revealed and will do his evil work (as described in 2:3-4). Why will God allow this evil man to act with unrestrained wickedness? To show people and nations their own sinfulness and to show them by bitter experience the true alternative to the lordship of Christ. People totally without God can act no better than vicious animals. Lawlessness, to a certain extent, is already going on, but the man of lawlessness has not yet come; he will *be revealed at the proper time*—that is, in God's time. Believers should not fear this time when the restraint is removed—God is far stronger than the man of lawlessness, and he will save his people.

2:8 **Then the man of lawlessness will be revealed, but the Lord Jesus will kill him with the breath of his mouth and destroy him by the splendor of his coming.**^{NLT} After the one who restrains rampant evil is removed, *then the man of lawlessness will be revealed.* For a period of time, he will have great power and act with notorious evil (as noted in 2:2-4). Just as this man of lawlessness will be revealed in God's timing, however, so he will also be destroyed. There will be an end to this man's evil. Indeed, when *the Lord Jesus* returns, he *will kill [the Antichrist] with the breath of his mouth.* This picture comes from Isaiah 11:4: "One breath from his mouth will destroy the wicked" (NLT). The picture of Christ "killing" this powerful evil man with a mere "breath" shows that between God and Satan there is no contest. No matter how powerful this evil man may become, he is no more than a flame to be blown out by the breath of the Lord.

A further picture is seen in the description that the man of lawlessness will be destroyed *by the splendor of [Christ's second] coming.* As a mere breath renders the Antichrist powerless, so the very appearance of Christ on the scene will ruin him. John describes this future appearance of Christ:

I saw heaven standing open and there before me was a white horse, whose rider is called Faithful and True. With justice he judges and makes war. His eyes are like blazing fire, and on his head are many crowns. He has a name written on him that no one knows but he himself. He is dressed in a robe dipped in blood, and his name is the Word of God. The armies of heaven were following him, riding on white horses and dressed in fine linen, white and clean. Out of his mouth comes a sharp sword

*with which to strike down the nations. "He will rule them with
an iron scepter." He treads the winepress of the fury of the
wrath of God Almighty. On his robe and on his thigh he has this
name written: KING OF KINGS AND LORD OF LORDS.* (Revelation
19:11-16 NIV)

Christ's title in this passage in Revelation indicates God's
sovereignty. Most of the world will be worshiping the beast, the
Antichrist, whom they will believe has all power and authority.
Then suddenly out of heaven will ride Christ—the King of kings
and Lord of lords—and his army of angels. His entrance will signal the end of the false powers.

2:9-10   **The coming of the lawless one will be in accordance with the
work of Satan displayed in all kinds of counterfeit miracles,
signs and wonders, and in every sort of evil that deceives
those who are perishing. They perish because they refused to
love the truth and so be saved.**NIV This verse answers the question that might have been plaguing the Thessalonians, and even
modern readers. How will this one man become so powerful?
How will he attain such notoriety and loyalty from the masses?
The answer is that this man will be Satan's tool, his *coming . . .
will be in accordance with the work of Satan* and will be *displayed in all kinds of counterfeit miracles, signs and wonders,
and in every sort of evil.* Jesus had warned that "false messiahs
and false prophets will rise up and perform great signs and
wonders so as to deceive, if possible, even God's chosen ones"
(Matthew 24:24 NLT). If even the numerous antichrists will have
extraordinary powers (1 John 2:18), this one who will be filled
with Satan's power will do signs that are even more extraordinary. When Jesus came, his ministry had "miracles, wonders, and
signs" (Acts 2:22 NLT). Jesus' followers were given power to do
"even greater things" (John 14:12 NIV), as evidenced by Paul's
miracle-working power (Romans 15:18-19; 2 Corinthians 12:12).
But while Jesus and his followers did miracles of compassion
for the purpose of bringing glory to God, the Antichrist will do
miracles characterized by evil and deceit for the purpose of bringing glory to himself.

The book of Revelation also describes the power that this evil
leader will have: "He did astounding miracles, even making fire
flash down to earth from the sky while everyone was watching.
And with all the miracles he was allowed to perform on behalf
of the first beast, [this is the answer to the above questions] he
deceived all the people who belong to this world. He ordered
the people to make a great statue of the first beast" (Revelation
13:13-14 NLT; see also Revelation 16:14; 19:20).

It will be this power *that deceives those who are perishing—* those who *refused to love the truth and so be saved.* The Christians will stand firm because they understand what is happening and will not be turned away. The statement that they *refused* the truth shows that at that point in time God's offer of salvation will still be available. The "truth" refers to the gospel message that offers salvation and eternal life to those who accept it. These people of the earth could turn away from this evil person and find eternal salvation in the truth of the gospel. The evil let loose upon the world will be used by God as a last chance for many. The choice will be crystal clear. Because the Antichrist will have taken over every other religion (2:4), the only two options will be to worship Christ or to worship the Antichrist. The unbelievers in the world will be so enamored of this powerful person that they will choose to follow him—away from God and into eternal death.

BEHIND THE SIGNS
This man of lawlessness will use counterfeit miracles, signs, and wonders to deceive and draw a following. Miracles from God can help strengthen our faith and lead people to Christ, but not all miracles are necessarily from God. Christ's miracles were significant not just because of their power but also because of their purpose—to help, to heal, and to point us to God. The man of lawlessness will have amazing power, but it will be from Satan. He will use this power to destroy and to lead people away from God and toward himself. If any so-called religious personality draws attention only to himself or herself, his or her work is not from God.

We need to use biblical principles to scrutinize those who become popular religious personalities or who have great authority. No Christian should be so gullible as to follow leaders who merely display power or have a following.

2:11 **For this reason God sends them a powerful delusion so that they will believe the lie.**[NIV] Those who make the choice to follow the Antichrist will be confirmed in that choice by God who *sends them a powerful delusion so that they will believe the lie.* They will continue to be deceived further and further—beyond simply believing the delusion—actively forwarding its cause. Again, the choice is made clear: over against "the truth" of the gospel (2:10) is *the lie* of the Antichrist, the truth that God is God versus the lie that the Antichrist is God. Satan also deludes: "The god of this age has blinded the minds of unbelievers, so that they cannot see the light of the gospel of the glory of Christ, who is the image of God" (2 Corinthians 4:4 NIV). God may use Satan as part of his

WARNING SIGNS OF DEVELOPING HARDNESS

Hardening is like a callus or like the tough bone fibers that bridge a fracture. Spiritual hardening begins with self-sufficiency, security in oneself, and self-satisfaction. The real danger is that at some point, repeated resistance to God will yield an actual inability to respond, which the Bible describes as a hardened heart. Insensitivity indicates advanced hardening. Here are some of the warning signs:

Warning Sign	Reference
Disobeying—Pharaoh's willful disobedience led to his hardened heart.	Exodus 4:21
Having wealth and prosperity—Taking God's blessings for granted can cause us to feel as if they were owed to us.	Deuteronomy 8:6-14
Rebelling and being discontented—Suffering or discomfort can create an attitude that blames God.	Psalm 95:8
Rejecting a deserved rebuke—Rejecting God's gift makes our neck stiff and our heart hard.	Proverbs 29:1
Refusing to listen—Refusing to listen leads to a loss of spiritual hearing.	Zechariah 7:11-13
Failing to respond—Listening to God with no intention of obeying produces an inability to obey.	Matthew 13:11-15

judgment on rebellion. That *God sends* this delusion shows his sovereignty in this entire event. At no point will God be out of control, even as Satan unleashes his power through the Antichrist. God's sovereignty is displayed in this way in Revelation 17:17: "For God has put a plan into their minds, a plan that will carry out his purposes. They will agree to give their authority to the scarlet beast, and so the words of God will be fulfilled" (NLT).

God will use the people's rebellion as a judgment against them. By their own free will they will choose to rebel. As condemnation on their sin, God will harden their hearts in unbelief, blinding them so that they can no longer respond to the truth. This is the horrible consequence of hardening hearts and serves as a warning to those who may be riding the fence between commitment to Christ and unbelief.

2:12 Then they will be condemned for enjoying evil rather than believing the truth.ᴺᴸᵀ The result of their choosing to "believe the lie" is that *they will be condemned.* The reason? For not *believing the truth* and for going so far down the path of evil that they don't even see it as evil; in fact, they are *enjoying evil.* The

path toward condemnation is downhill and slippery. It begins
with a fascination with evil and leads to an acceptance of a lie
and simultaneous rejection of the truth—powerful delusions that
lead one deeper into evil so that it is accepted and even enjoyed.
At that point, people's hearts are hardened against God and his
Word, for they do not feel any need for either.

GOD VS. EVIL
Does God blind people to the truth? To understand God's using
a powerful delusion or "blinding" in his judgment, one must
first understand God's nature. (1) God himself is good (Psalm
11:7). (2) God created a good world that fell because of man's
sin (Romans 5:12). (3) Someday God will re-create the world
and it will be good again (Revelation 21:1). (4) God is stronger
than evil (Matthew 13:41-43; Revelation 19:11-21). (5) God
allows evil and thus has control over it. God did not create evil,
and he offers help to those who wish to overcome it (Matthew
11:28-30). (6) God uses everything—both good and evil—for his
good purposes (Genesis 50:20; Romans 8:28).

The Bible reveals a God who hates all evil and will one day do
away with it completely and forever (Revelation 20:10-15). God
does not entice anyone to become evil. Those committed to evil,
however, may be used by God to sin even more in order to has-
ten their deserved judgment (see Exodus 11:10). We don't need
to understand every detail of how God works in order to have
perfect confidence in his absolute power over evil and his total
goodness toward us.

BELIEVERS SHOULD STAND FIRM / 2:13-17

Having just painted the picture of the world with the undercurrent
of evil waiting to be unleashed, and a period of time when evil
will reign and people will worship it, Paul countered by encouraging believers to stand firm in their faith. Every passage in the
New Testament about the Lord's return ends with ethical man-
dates such as those found in this section and in chapter 3.

2:13 **As for us, we can't help but thank God for you, dear brothers
and sisters loved by the Lord. We are always thankful that
God chose you to be among the first to experience salvation—
a salvation that came through the Spirit who makes you holy
and through your belief in the truth.**ᴺᴸᵀ Once again, Paul and
his companions paused to *thank God* for what he had done and
was continuing to do through the Thessalonian believers. In
contrast to people who will rebel against God and face eternal
destruction, those who believe have a glorious future. *God chose*

[the Thessalonian believers] to be among *the first to experience salvation;* they were among the early believers, the first in Thessalonica, and they had been chosen by God for that special privilege. Paul consistently taught that salvation begins and ends with God. People can do nothing to be saved on their own merit—all must accept God's gift of salvation. There is no other way to receive forgiveness from sin. Paul was encouraging the Thessalonian believers by reminding them that they had been chosen by God from the beginning. Present and future persecution and suffering should not lead to panic. Instead, believers should stand firm. Their faith should be in the One who will win the battle. He can be trusted to bring them to heaven, no matter what happens on earth.

Salvation comes to those who believe *in the truth*—that is, they accept the gospel message of salvation through Christ. Then a process begins by which believers are made *holy* like Christ. This is called "sanctification." This is a gradual, lifelong process that will be completed when believers see Christ face-to-face. "Beloved, we are God's children now; what we will be has not yet been revealed. What we do know is this: when he is revealed, we will be like him, for we will see him as he is" (1 John 3:2 NRSV).

2:14 He called you to this through our gospel, that you might share in the glory of our Lord Jesus Christ.NIV God's "call" came to these Thessalonians through his human emissaries, Paul and his companions. God worked through Paul, Silas, Timothy, and others to tell the Good News to the Thessalonians so *that [they] might share in the glory of our Lord Jesus Christ.* The Thessalonians were facing persecution for their faith; Paul had just finished describing a time on earth of even more intense persecution. There was no doubt about the outcome. Those who believe will share in Christ's glory when he comes to restore justice on the earth (see 1:5-10). Believers will reflect his glory back to him as they praise him.

The system has not changed. God still invites people through the simple gospel message of salvation through faith in Jesus Christ. And that gospel message is presented by other human beings who have experienced God's grace. The privilege of all believers is to take that message into a lost and sinful world and find others to join them in glorifying Christ.

2:15 With all these things in mind, dear brothers and sisters, stand firm and keep a strong grip on everything we taught you both in person and by letter.NLT Paul knew that the Thessalonians would face pressure from persecution, false teachers, worldliness, and apathy to waver from the truth and to leave the faith. *With all these things in mind,* Paul urged them to *stand firm and keep* *a strong grip on everything* that Paul and his companions had taught. The Thessalonians had received much teaching in person, and they had Paul's letters. They would need to hold on to the truth they had been taught.

It will take faith to hold on when persecution becomes intense; it will be important to continue to work for God no matter what happens (see Mark 13:13; Hebrews 3:6). Just because Christians are saved and certain of victory doesn't mean that they can sit out during the battle. Their own salvation does not excuse them from working to bring others to faith in Christ. They will need to be braced and ready, with all their armor on (Ephesians 6:13-18), but they are not alone. They can draw strength from other believers and know that the Holy Spirit will give them inner confidence.

A STRONG GRIP
How do we "stand firm and keep a strong grip"? We should hold on to the truth of Christ's teachings because our lives depend on it.

To believe in Jesus and stand firm will take perseverance because our faith will be challenged and opposed. Severe trials will sift true Christians from fair-weather believers. Enduring to the end does not earn salvation for us but marks us as already saved. The assurance of our salvation will keep us going through times of persecution.

Because Christ lives in us, we can remain courageous and hopeful to the end. Without this enduring faithfulness, we could easily be blown away by the winds of temptation, false teaching, or persecution.

2:16-17 **May our Lord Jesus Christ himself and God our Father, who loved us and by his grace gave us eternal encouragement and good hope, encourage your hearts and strengthen you in every good deed and word.**[NIV] This prayer is similar to the one at the end of the main section of his first letter (1 Thessalonians 3:11-13). Notice that Paul gave the full title of the *Lord Jesus Christ,* showing his majesty and power. God is called *our Father* and the following words, "his grace," are singular, showing that Jesus and God are really one person. Through that grace—undeserved kindness—God and Christ *gave . . . eternal encouragement and good hope* to the believers. Christianity is not a faith of questions and worries—not a faith in which believers must wait until the end to see if they will make it. Instead, believers are given hope and encouragement through the certainty of God's promises.

It always helps, however, to pray for believers everywhere,

especially those facing persecution for their faith, that God would *encourage [their] hearts and strengthen [them] in every good deed and word.* The encouragement of hearts gives inner conviction; the good deeds and words reveal that inner conviction to the world.

ETERNAL ENCOURAGEMENT
Even the strongest people get tired at times, but God's power and strength never diminish. He is never too tired or too busy to help and listen. When you feel all of life crushing you and you cannot go another step, remember that you can call upon the Lord Jesus Christ to renew your strength.

Hoping in the Lord means expecting that his promise of strength will help us to rise above life's distractions and difficulties. It also means trusting God and his Word. Depend on God as your source of encouragement.

---

2 Thessalonians 3

Paul had been writing about the future, describing the coming of the Antichrist and the future days of rebellion and lawlessness. That man of evil has not yet come because he is being held back. Yet, even so, Paul stated that "the secret power of lawlessness is already at work" (2:7 NIV). Evil is at work in the world, but it is also being held in check. What does that mean for Christians? How then are they to live in this present evil world as they are preparing for the next?

3:1 Finally, brothers and sisters, pray for us, so that the word of the Lord may spread rapidly and be glorified everywhere, just as it is among you.NRSV Paul prayed regularly for the believers in the various churches, and he did not hesitate to ask for their prayers in return (see the chart "Paul's Prayers" in 1 Thessalonians 1:1, page 14). So here, as he prepared to offer final words of advice to the *brothers and sisters* in Thessalonica, he first asked them to pray for him and his fellow missionaries (the Greek word means "keep on praying"). The focus of Paul's desire was *that the word of the Lord may spread rapidly and be glorified everywhere, just as it is among you.* The "word of the Lord" as used here may be contrasted with the word of the false teachers (2:2, 15), and it refers to preaching of the gospel. The Greek word for "spread rapidly" *(treche)* literally pictures a runner, perhaps like one who would participate in races in the Isthmian Games held in Corinth (from where Paul was writing). Paul saw the gospel message "running" across the known world, finding converts in every place, just as it had in Thessalonica. The preaching of the gospel would result in honor being given to the Lord because of the marvelous results in the lives of those who believe. The Thessalonians had been an exemplary congregation (1 Thessalonians 1:6-10). Paul wanted them to pray for God's power to intervene in other places so that many would be saved and God would be glorified.

3:2 And that we may be rescued from wicked and evil people; for not all have faith.NRSV In addition to praying for more converts, Paul asked the believers to also pray *that we may be rescued from* *wicked and evil people.* As the gospel message advances, it always faces severe opposition. The spiritual battle rages intensely for people's souls, and Satan does not easily let go of his own. Thus, the missionaries would need prayer for safety. If Paul asked for it, how much more should believers today pray for one another as they seek to share the gospel message—whether across the street or across the world. In Greek, the phrase "wicked and evil people" has a definite article, so Paul was referring to a particular group, perhaps some of his detractors there in Corinth (see Acts 18:12). These people were "wicked and evil" because they did *not . . . have faith.* In Greek the word has a definite article, "the faith," referring to the Christian faith. But as it is used here, it most likely refers to faith or faithfulness, meaning a believing response to the gospel. Paul's enemies were those who did not believe in the gospel message and were actively working against it.

> Prayer is a powerful thing, for God has bound and tied himself thereto. None can believe how powerful prayer is, and what it is able to effect, but those who have learned it by experience.
>
> *Martin Luther*

PRAYER POWER
Beneath the surface of the routine of daily life, a fierce struggle between invisible spiritul powers rages. Our main defense is prayer that God will protect us from the evil one and the he will strengthen us. We will need the full armor of God as we face spiritual attacks and we will be attacked, for Christians are Satan's prime targets, his avowed enemies.

The following guidelines can help you prepare for and survive satanic attacks:

- Take the threat of spiritual attack seriously.
- Pray for strength and help from God.
- Study the Bible to recognize Satan's style and tactics.
- Memorize Scripture so it will be a source of help no matter where you are.
- Associate with those who speak the truth.
- Practice what you are taught by spiritual leaders.

3:3 But the Lord is faithful, and he will strengthen and protect you from the evil one.[NIV] There is a play on words in verses 2 and 3: "Faith" in 3:2 is *pistis;* "faithful" in this verse is *pistos.* While many people may be without faith, that does not change the fact that *the Lord is faithful.* As at the end of his first letter (1 Thessalonians 5:24), Paul reminded the believers of God's faithfulness: God can be depended upon to keep his promises, he is loyal, and he is constant. (See the chart "God Is Faithful" on pages 90–91 for verses in both the Old and New Testaments that describe God's everlasting faithfulness.) Because God will not change, neither will his faithfulness to his promises.

Because of that faithfulness, God *will strengthen and protect you from the evil one.* As the spiritual battle intensifies, the true enemy of all believers is really only one person—the "evil one," Satan himself. Because the Lord is faithful, he will protect his gospel message, and it will continue to spread across the world and achieve results. Because the Lord is faithful, he will strengthen and protect the believers. This does not mean that they will never face difficulties; it just means that God is faithful. Although there have been and will be persecutions, death, difficulties, suffering, problems, and even failing churches, there will be no ultimate defeat because God has already won the war. Neither the Word nor the church will fail—because God is faithful. Through any situation, God can be depended upon to strengthen and protect his people. The result for all believers will be eternity with God. That promise will never change.

Yet even so, prayer is a vital factor behind all of this activity. As the missionaries spread God's message, they understood that spiritual forces were at work—the faithful Lord with them, the evil one against them. They realized that they were not involved in a merely human endeavor; they were on the Lord's battlefields, under his command, with his authority, knowing they would win, yet needing his guidance and the constant prayers of believers every step of the way.

3:4 And we have confidence in the Lord concerning you, that you are doing and will go on doing the things that we command.NRSV Christ is faithful, but his followers must do their part in being obedient. Paul had *confidence in the Lord concerning* the Thessalonians. His confidence rested not in the Thessalonians themselves but in God who had chosen them. They had more than shown their obedience to the teachings of the apostles, even as they had experienced persecution. Paul knew that God would strengthen them so that they could do and *go on doing the things that [he commanded].* Believers at this time did not have the New Testament, so they had to listen carefully to the teachings of the apostles; therefore, Paul spoke of them doing what he and the other apostles did *command* because their teaching came from God. This principle of imitation is taught also in 3:7, 9.

> Faith and obedience are bound up in the same bundle. He that obeys God, trusts God; and he that trusts God, obeys God.
>
> *Charles H. Spurgeon*

Paul may have been referring to the specific command to pray, which he had just mentioned in the previous verses, or, more likely, these words are a prelude to the following verses that give practical advice regarding living out the faith (Paul used the word "command" again in 3:6).

3:5 **May the Lord direct your hearts into God's love and Christ's perseverance.**^{NIV} Paul's prayer for these believers was that *the Lord* would *direct [their] hearts.* "Direct" means to keep their hearts loyal to him or to incline their hearts toward God by removing obstacles from the path. Wanting the believers to move forward with commitment, Paul asked God to guide the believers as they meditated on God's love for them and on Christ's patient steadfastness. Such inner determination would enable them to face and overcome their difficulties.

REFLECTING AND FOCUSING
Christ endured great suffering for us. As a result, he can be an inspiring example for believers who face suffering and persecution. Christ was ridiculed, whipped, beaten, spit upon, and crucified. Even so, he did not give in to fatigue, discouragement, or despair.

By focusing on Christ and what he did on our behalf, we won't become weary and give up. Trials can cause us to become discouraged and even to despair. During these difficult times, we can remember how Christ endured and be inspired. Throughout the history of the church, meditation on the suffering of Christ has helped countless martyrs and prisoners. Christ's suffering surpassed any suffering we might face. Facing hardship and discouragement, we must not lose sight of the big picture. We are not alone; Jesus stands with us.

PAUL ADMONISHES THE CHURCH AGAINST LAZINESS / 3:6-15

Besides the Second Coming, the topic of laziness among believers takes up the most space in this letter. The fact that Paul had already discussed this in his first letter (see 1 Thessalonians 5:14) shows that the problem had not been solved but had continued. This caused Paul great concern, so he gave stern commands.

3:6 **And now, dear brothers and sisters, we give you this command in the name of our Lord Jesus Christ: Stay away from all believers who live idle lives and don't follow the tradition they received from us.**^{NLT} Paul had already discussed the issue of idle Christians in the first letter, but apparently the problem had continued (1 Thessalonians 5:14). Perhaps Paul's instruction had not been strong enough, so this passage made it clear that his commands regarding idleness came *in the name of our Lord Jesus Christ.* The first letter tells Christians to "warn those who are lazy" (1 Thessalonians 5:14 NLT); that is, the believers were to firmly admonish those who were *atakta,* a word used for soldiers who would not stay in the ranks. While everyone else was working and serving, they would not. Some were using the excuse of waiting for Christ to return. They may have considered work too menial or unspiritual, equivalent to laying up treasures on earth rather than in heaven. They may have been creating a problem by expecting wealthier people in the church to support them. But Paul was firm that these believers were not honoring their faith.

BREAK TIME
Paul wrote about the lazy person. Paul explained that when he and his companions were in Thessalonica, they worked hard, buying what they needed rather than becoming a burden to any of the believers. The rule they followed was, "Those unwilling to work will not get to eat" (3:10 NLT). There's a difference between leisure and laziness. Relaxation and recreation provide a necessary and much-needed balance to our lives. When it is time to work, however, Christians should jump right in, making the most of their talent and time, doing all they can to provide for themselves and their dependents. Rest when you should be resting, and work when you should be working.

This letter goes a step further in his command regarding these people. No longer are believers told to "warn" these lazy people; they are told to *stay away from all believers who live idle lives and don't follow the tradition they received from us.* Apparently the warnings had not been heeded by these lazy people, so Paul would give them another command in 3:12. Yet he told the believers to "stay away" from them. This refers not to excommunication from the church but to withdrawing intimate fellowship from them. By refusing to associate with these people, the Christians were rebuking them, hoping to get them to change their conduct. Basically, Paul was saying, "Cut off their support!" These lazy people, as noted in 3:11, were "refusing to work and . . . meddling in other people's business" (NLT). In the spirit of love, the best way to deal with these meddlers is to not talk to them—not give them anything to meddle in! When they find themselves with nothing to do and no hearing for their meddling, they will hopefully find a more constructive use for their time.

By contrast, Paul and his companions had worked hard when they were in Thessalonica. In addition to teaching the gospel, they had "toiled to earn a living so that [they] would not be a burden to any of [them]" (1 Thessalonians 2:9 NLT). Paul and his companions had a right to expect support for their ministry, but they had chosen instead to work hard and to be a good example to the believers.

GOOD EXAMPLES
The New Testament places strong emphasis on imitating leaders. It also gives strong words to leaders that they be worthy of emulation. As a Christian you owe much to others who have taught you and who have modeled for you right Christian living. Continue following the good examples of those who have invested themselves in you by investing your life through evangelism, service, and Christian education. You also must become a model worth emulating. (The following Scripture verses are quoted from the NIV.)

- Matthew 11:29: "Take my yoke upon you and learn from me."
- Philippians 3:17: "Join with others in following my example."
- 1 Thessalonians 1:6-7: "You became imitators of us and of the Lord. . . . And so you became a model to all the believers."
- 2 Thessalonians 3:9: "We did this . . . to make ourselves a model for you to follow."
- 1 Timothy 1:16: "In me . . . Christ Jesus might display his unlimited patience as an example for those who would believe on him."
- 1 Peter 2:21: "To this you were called, because Christ suffered for you, leaving you an example, that you should follow in his steps."
- 1 Peter 5:3: "Not lording it over those entrusted to you, but being examples to the flock."
(See also 1 Corinthians 4:16 and Hebrews 6:12.)

3:7-8 **For you yourselves know how you ought to imitate us; we were not idle when we were with you, and we did not eat anyone's bread without paying for it; but with toil and labor we worked night and day, so that we might not burden any of you.**[NRSV] Paul's first letter describes how he and his companions had worked during their stay in Thessalonica. They had not been *idle* as these believers were and had not taken food *without paying for it.* They did not want to be a *burden* to anyone but wanted to pay their own way. Paul and his companions probably enjoyed hospitality at various times during their ministry; Paul's point was that he did not expect hospitality or impose it on anyone. They had paid for their lodging and their food in Jason's home (Acts 17:7) *with toil and labor [and they] worked night and day.*

Paul had been trained as a tent maker (Acts 18:3), and he had worked at this job even as he preached the gospel, taught, and built up a body of believers in this city. Because the people who had brought the gospel to the Thessalonians had worked to not be a burden on anyone, so should the new believers in the city *imitate* that example.

3:9 We did this, not because we do not have the right to such help, but in order to make ourselves a model for you to follow.^NIV Paul had made this same point in 1 Thessalonians 2:7. Paul and the other missionaries had *the right to such help;* that is, they had a right to expect lodging and

> Work is the natural exercise and function of man. . . . Work is not primarily a thing one does to live, but the thing one lives to do. It is, or should be, the full expression of the worker's faculties, the thing in which he finds spiritual, mental and bodily satisfaction, and the medium in which he offers himself to God.
>
> *Dorothy L. Sayers*

food in exchange for the message they had brought (see Luke 10:7; 1 Corinthians 9:7-14). Most traveling preachers did this, depending for their livelihood on the generosity of their listeners. Paul did not want to be a burden, however, nor did he want to appear to be preaching in order to be housed and fed. In some places he did accept such gifts, but in Thessalonica he did not. So strong was his passion for spreading the gospel message that he would not allow anything to hinder its progress. If it seemed that to accept food and lodging would hinder his effectiveness as a minister of the gospel, then he would gladly waive his rights and work to pay his way. In this way, the missionaries had made themselves *a model for [the believers] to follow.* Those who share the gospel message with others must not only speak the message but live it as well; they must be examples worthy of imitation.

3:10 For even when we were with you, we gave you this command: Anyone unwilling to work should not eat.^NRSV Not only had Paul and Silas been an example of Christian living to the Thessalonians, but they had also explained clearly what was expected. The *command* regarding laziness had been given right from the start—*even when* the missionaries were with the new believers, teaching them. They had said at that time: *Anyone unwilling to work should not eat.* The saying may have been coined anywhere and may have been a common theme among laborers as they worked together or as they trained apprentices. Paul applied it to the Christian life to show believers that laziness, in any form, would not be acceptable. Because Christians are known for their kindness, sharing of their goods with one another, and willingness to take care of people, some might want to take advantage of them. Paul sternly reprimanded such thinking. Those "unwilling" to work—that is, those who refuse to work when they are able and when there is work to be done—should not then be given food so they can eat. If they can earn money for their food, they should do so without depending on others to care for them.

Be careful not to use this verse on those who are willing but unable to work. It is easy to glibly dismiss the difficult conditions of those with disabilities, lack of job training, or lack of job availability. Paul's harsh words are for people who are unwilling to work when they have both the ability and the opportunity. This phrase should not to be used to hammer the poor.

AUTHORITY
When Paul issued a command, such as in 3:11-12, he did so with the authority of Jesus Christ. Only those who had witnessed the resurrection of Christ and had been given this authority could use that authority. In Galatians 4:14, Paul commended the Galatian believers for welcoming him as if he were Jesus Christ.

Today, no individual or group can claim that same authority. Our authority is God's Word and the example of Christ himself. At times, leaders in some churches or groups demand total submission and obedience. We need to stay away from those kinds of authoritarian structures. Instead, leaders must take Peter's advice: "Don't lord it over the people assigned to your care, but lead them by your own good example" (1 Peter 5:3 NLT).

3:11-12 **We hear that some among you are idle. They are not busy; they are busybodies. Such people we command and urge in the Lord Jesus Christ to settle down and earn the bread they eat.**[NIV] Here is the reason for Paul's hard-hitting words on this topic of laziness. *We hear,* he wrote. Word had reached Paul in Corinth that some of the believers in Thessalonica were *idle*— meaning that they were refusing to work. So Paul was not the only one concerned about this issue; the believers in Thessalonica had felt that it was so important that they had notified Paul. Perhaps they had taken Paul's advice in the first letter but had seen no results, so they wanted him to deal directly with these people.

It is possible that these idle people were being idle for "spiritual" reasons. Some people in the Thessalonian church were falsely teaching that because Christ would return any day, people should set aside their responsibilities, quit work, do no future planning, and just wait for the Lord. Or they may have thought that labor was beneath them and wanted to spend their time being spiritual. But not being *busy* only made them *busybodies.* Instead of working, they were minding other people's business, prying into the private lives of others and interfering with their progress. Some were persuading others to adopt their point of view on the Second Coming. Their lack of activity was leading them into sin. They had become a burden to the church, which was supporting them; they were wasting time that could have been used for helping others.

These church members may have thought that they were being more spiritual by not working, but Paul sternly commanded and urged them *to settle down and earn the bread they eat.* Apparently these busybodies were "meddling in other people's business" (3:11 NLT) and then were eating other people's hard-earned food. Paul did not mince words with these people. Because they were all brothers and sisters in the faith, they were all responsible for one another—not to care for lazy people but to work hard so that everyone would be cared for. That Paul made these commands *in the Lord Jesus* reveals his understanding of his authority as an apostle, as a personal representative of the Lord himself.

FAITH AND WORKS
Paul stressed good works. As the apostle of faith, he had much to say about works, and not all of it was negative. Paul taught that faith must come before works but that genuine faith always leads to works of obedience (see Romans 2:6-11; 13:12-14; 14:12; 2 Corinthians 5:6-10; Galatians 6:2-10; Ephesians 2:8-10; Colossians 3:1-10). Paul made it clear that we are saved by grace through faith, but with an expected result: "It is by grace you have been saved, through faith—and this not from yourselves, it is the gift of God—not by works, so that no one can boast. For we are God's workmanship, created in Christ Jesus to do good works, which God prepared in advance for us to do" (Ephesians 2:8-10 NIV). We are not saved *by* works, but we are saved *to do* good works. Don't give up, no matter how tiresome the work or annoying the recipients.

3:13 **As for the rest of you, dear brothers and sisters, never get tired of doing good.**[NLT] To those hardworking believers, those who were not lazy, Paul said, *Never get tired of doing good.* In contrast to the idlers who had persisted in their idleness even since Paul's last letter, these hardworking believers should not let the idlers cause them to become dispirited in their work. Paul had written almost the same thing to the Galatians: "Let us not become weary in doing good, for at the proper time we will reap a harvest if we do not give up" (Galatians 6:9 NIV). Paul knew

that the believers could become discouraged when they tried
to do right and received no word of thanks or saw no tangible
results. But Paul challenged all of the believers to keep on doing
good and to trust God for the results.

CHURCH DISCIPLINE
Many New Testament passages concerning discipline in the
church stress love and restoration (see 1 Corinthians 4:14;
Galatians 6:1; James 5:16). The goal is not to punish the person
but to bring the offender back to Christ. Second Thessalonians
3:14-15 contains important information regarding church discipline. How should the church handle a person who is guilty of
inappropriate behavior?

Focus
- Focus only on the inappropriate behavior.
- Don't ignore that behavior.
- Determine to take care of the matter in private—perhaps that
  will be all that is needed.

Action
- In Thessalonica, the lazy people had disregarded Paul's
  warning in his first letter (1 Thessalonians 5:14), so Paul
  told the other believers not even to associate with these lazy
  people (2 Thessalonians 3:14-15). (See also 1 Corinthians
  5:9, 11.)
- The action should be taken by the whole church (Matthew
  18:17). This also keeps factions and divisions from forming.
  In the case of inappropriate behavior (as opposed to sin and
  adamant refusal to stop sinning), Paul counseled not excommunication but withdrawal of fellowship.

Attitude
- The correction should be given in an attitude of gentleness
  (Galatians 6:1).
- The person should not be regarded as an enemy—that would
  be excommunication. Instead, he or she should be counseled
  and warned.

Goal
- The purpose of this disciplinary action is not retribution but
  restoration. The desire is to win the brother or sister back into
  the fellowship.
- The point is to have the brother or sister reflect on the inappropriate behavior, understand why it is inappropriate, and
  make the necessary changes.

  (See also Matthew 18:15-20 and 1 Corinthians 5:1-13 for
  more on church discipline.)

3:14-15   **Take note of those who refuse to obey what we say in this
letter. Stay away from them so they will be ashamed. Don't
think of them as enemies, but warn them as you would a**

brother or sister.ᴺᴸᵀ At the same time that the believers were
not to get weary of doing good, they also were not to put up
with fellow believers who were being disobedient to Paul's commands regarding laziness. The believers who were working hard
and following Paul's commands were not expected to support
the lazy people in the name of "doing good." So Paul repeated
his direction regarding this issue: *Take note of those who refuse
to obey. . . . Stay away from them* (see 3:6). The hope was that
the idle people would become *ashamed* of their actions and
finally become so hungry (when no one would support and feed
them) that they would be forced back to work. Paul counseled
the church to stop supporting financially and associating with
those who persisted in their idleness. Hunger and loneliness can
be very effective ways to make the idle person become produc-
tive. Paul was not advising coldness or cruelty, for these people
were not *enemies.* They were misguided and mistaken, but they
were not to be thrown out of the church. They did need a good
dose of tough love, however—the kind of love that should be
shown to *a brother or sister.* Verbal warnings had apparently not
been enough, for Paul had already offered that in his first letter
(1 Thessalonians 5:14); now the warnings would be acted out
physically.

PAUL'S FINAL GREETINGS / 3:16-18

Paul knew that the church would need to deal with false teaching regarding the Second Coming (as discussed in chapter 2)
and with those members who were not living as they should (as
discussed in chapter 3). Paul had issued teachings and commands,
but the believers would have to carry them out. In his closing
words, Paul prayed for peace for the church so that it could
handle these issues and then continue strong in the work of the
kingdom.

3:16 **Now may the Lord of peace himself give you peace at all times
in all ways. The Lord be with all of you.**ᴺᴿˢⱽ Just as Paul began
his letter with "grace and peace" (1:2 NLT), so he ended it (see
3:18). At the end of his first letter, Paul had prayed for the Thessalonians that the "God of peace" would sanctify them (1 Thessalonians 5:23 NLT). He knew that the commands he had given
would take more than human effort alone to fulfill. It would be
difficult for the idle people to humbly go back to work; it would
be difficult for the annoyed believers to treat these people lov-
ingly yet with a firm hand. Paul did not expect them to do this in
their own strength, however, so he prayed that *the Lord of peace*

himself would give them *peace at all times in all ways.* Paul referred to "the God of peace" or "the Lord of peace" often at the end of his letters (see Romans 15:33; 16:20; 2 Corinthians 13:11; Philippians 4:9). The peace God gives does not mean absence of conflict (see John 14:27; 16:33). The peace God gives is confident assurance in any circumstance, with no fear of the present or the future. Not only did the believers have peace, but they also had the Lord himself, for he would be with them through his Spirit.

3:17 I, Paul, write this greeting in my own hand, which is the distinguishing mark in all my letters. This is how I write.NIV Usually Paul dictated his letters to a scribe, but often he would end the letter with a note in his own handwriting (see also 1 Corinthians 16:21; Galatians 6:11; Colossians 4:18; Philemon 1:19). This assured the recipients that false teachers were not writing letters in Paul's name—which was a concern in Thessalonica (see 2:2). It also gave the letters a personal touch.

3:18 May the grace of our Lord Jesus Christ be with you all.NLT Paul often closed his letters with a prayer of *grace* for the believers. This closing is identical to his first letter (1 Thessalonians 5:28). Paul wanted his readers to continue to experience *the grace of our Lord Jesus Christ.* "Grace" is undeserved favor from God to his people. This grace from God would help believers in their daily walk with him.

SUFFERING SAINTS
This book is especially meaningful for those who are being persecuted or are under pressure because of their faith. In chapter 1 we are told what suffering can do for us. In chapter 2 we are assured of final victory. In chapter 3 we are encouraged to continue living responsibly in spite of difficult circumstances. Christ's return is more than a doctrine; it is a promise. It is not just for the future; it has a vital impact on how we live now.

BIBLIOGRAPHY

Bruce, F. F. *1 and 2 Thessalonians* in Word Biblical Commentary Series. Waco, Tex.: Word, 1982.

Douglas, J. D., ed. *The New Greek-English Interlinear New Testament.* Translated by Robert K. Brown and Philip W. Comfort. Wheaton, Ill.: Tyndale House, 1990.

Hawthorne, Gerald, Ralph Martin, and Daniel Reid. *Dictionary of Paul and His Letters.* Downers Grove, Ill.: InterVarsity Press, 1993.

Morris, Leon. *The First and Second Epistles to the Thessalonians.* The New International Commentary on the New Testament. Grand Rapids: Eerdmans, 1991 (revised edition).

Morris, Leon. *1 and 2 Thessalonians.* Tyndale New Testament Commentaries. Grand Rapids: Eerdmans, 1984.

Stott, John. *The Gospel and the End of Time.* Downers Grove, Ill.: InterVarsity Press, 1991.

Thomas, Robert L. "1 and 2 Thessalonians" in *The Expositor's Bible Commentary.* Vol. 11. Edited by Frank E. Gaebelein. Grand Rapids: Zondervan, 1978.

INDEX